Number 136
Winter 2012

New Directions for Evaluation

Sandra Mathison
Editor-in-Chief

Evaluation Advisory Groups

Ross VeLure Roholt
Michael L. Baizerman
Editors

EVALUATION ADVISORY GROUPS
Ross VeLure Roholt, Michael L. Baizerman (eds.)
New Directions for Evaluation, no. 136
Sandra Mathison, Editor-in-Chief

Microfilm copies of issues and articles are available in 16mm and 35mm, as well as microfiche in 105mm, through University Microfilms Inc., 300 North Zeeb Road, Ann Arbor, MI 48106-1346.

New Directions for Evaluation is indexed in Education Research Complete (EBSCO), ERIC Database (Education Resources Information Center), Higher Education Abstracts (Claremont Graduate University), SCOPUS (Elsevier), Social Services Abstracts (CSA/CIG), Sociological Abstracts (CSA/CIG), and Worldwide Political Science Abstracts (CSA/CIG).

NEW DIRECTIONS FOR EVALUATION (ISSN 1097-6736, electronic ISSN 1534-875X) is part of The Jossey-Bass Education Series and is published quarterly by Wiley Subscription Services, Inc., A Wiley Company, at Jossey-Bass, One Montgomery Street, Suite 1200, San Francisco, CA 94104-4594.

SUBSCRIPTIONS for individuals cost $89 for U.S./Canada/Mexico; $113 international. For institutions, $313 U.S.; $353 Canada/Mexico; $387 international. Electronic only: $89 for individuals all regions; $313 for institutions all regions. Print and electronic: $98 for individuals in the U.S., Canada, and Mexico; $122 for individuals for the rest of the world; $363 for institutions in the U.S.; $403 for institutions in Canada and Mexico; $437 for institutions for the rest of the world.

EDITORIAL CORRESPONDENCE should be addressed to the Editor-in-Chief, Sandra Mathison, University of British Columbia, 2125 Main Mall, Vancouver, BC V6T 1Z4, Canada.

www.josseybass.com

Editorial Policy and Procedures

New Directions for Evaluation, a quarterly sourcebook, is an official publication of the American Evaluation Association. The journal publishes empirical, methodological, and theoretical works on all aspects of evaluation. A reflective approach to evaluation is an essential strand to be woven through every issue. The editors encourage issues that have one of three foci: (1) craft issues that present approaches, methods, or techniques that can be applied in evaluation practice, such as the use of templates, case studies, or survey research; (2) professional issues that present topics of import for the field of evaluation, such as utilization of evaluation or locus of evaluation capacity; (3) societal issues that draw out the implications of intellectual, social, or cultural developments for the field of evaluation, such as the women's movement, communitarianism, or multiculturalism. A wide range of substantive domains is appropriate for *New Directions for Evaluation;* however, the domains must be of interest to a large audience within the field of evaluation. We encourage a diversity of perspectives and experiences within each issue, as well as creative bridges between evaluation and other sectors of our collective lives.

The editors do not consider or publish unsolicited single manuscripts. Each issue of the journal is devoted to a single topic, with contributions solicited, organized, reviewed, and edited by a guest editor. Issues may take any of several forms, such as a series of related chapters, a debate, or a long article followed by brief critical commentaries. In all cases, the proposals must follow a specific format, which can be obtained from the editor-in-chief. These proposals are sent to members of the editorial board and to relevant substantive experts for peer review. The process may result in acceptance, a recommendation to revise and resubmit, or rejection. However, the editors are committed to working constructively with potential guest editors to help them develop acceptable proposals.

Sandra Mathison, Editor-in-Chief
University of British Columbia
2125 Main Mall
Vancouver, BC V6T 1Z4
CANADA
e-mail: nde@eval.org

CONTENTS

EDITORS' NOTES

In professional life, advice often is technical, an answer to a question, or perspectival, another way for seeing a problem or for working towards a solution. From the everyday to the technical, there are multiple advice systems and cultures, each with its own social and cultural rules and protocols, from the informal and mundane, such as where to get the best pizza around here, to the formal and exotic, such as how to best draw a sample of cancer patients for an evaluation of posttreatment recovery. Asking and giving advice works to bind and bond us socially, to thoughts, perspectives, ideas, opinions, beliefs, and expertise—to others. In religious work and in the university, the advice system of asking and proffering thoughts, opinions, preferences, and other types of advice serves to join the asker and answerer to larger ideas, worlds, histories, and cultures.

In evaluation work, advice solicitation and response are both mundane practices and formal structures, both dropping in on a colleague to get his or her opinion and organizing and using a formal evaluation advisory (EAG) or consultation (ECG) group (the latter is the preferred term in U.S. Federal service because of statute). It is the formal structure and how it can be used to enhance the quality of an evaluation that are the foci of this issue. But why devote a full issue to advisory groups if asking and receiving advice is so ordinary a process? Is it not also a common professional evaluation practice?

It may well be an everyday evaluation practice—there are no known surveys—and although the literature increasingly refers to the value of using outside advice for enhancing evaluation quality and the use of findings, this practice is neither fully analyzed nor theorized deeply, with Patton (2008) an exception. This issue intends both locating what the editors call the *advice system* in historical, social, and cultural contexts and then using several perspectives to explicate formal advice structures and practices, bringing in consultation as a cousin of advice. Case studies ground these analytic and theoretical overviews, with stories about everyday, intentional practice in organizing and using formal and informal advisory structures and advisory practices. Examples include Indigenous community members as technical, cultural advisors (Johnston-Goodstar), a variety of community-based local residents (Cohen), advisory groups in everyday evaluation practice (Mattessich), a variety of advisory group protocols (Compton and Baizerman), the use of an advisory group for a contested Northern Ireland museum exhibit (VeLure Roholt), a youth advisory group within a community foundation (Richards-Schuster), and the concerns and questions about why to have and how to work with an EAG/ECG. Taken

NEW DIRECTIONS FOR EVALUATION, no. 136, Winter 2012 © Wiley Periodicals, Inc., and the American Evaluation Association. Published online in Wiley Online Library (wileyonlinelibrary.com) • DOI: 10.1002/ev.20030

together, the range, richness, and utility of an advisory structure strategy and practice become clear.

Evaluation is part of an advice system when the evaluator, contractor, and/or others intend a study to be used for program improvement, accountability, policy, decision making, and the like; that is, when it is intended to be used. It is in its use-purpose that evaluation can be clearly contrasted to the social and behavioral sciences (Mathison, 2008). When in their applied form, a claim to practicality is made then that these too can be part of the advice system—how? By providing data and derivative ideas, suggestions, and recommendations for action, that is program improvement and the rest. The metaphor "what do the data say?" is one basis for advice; a second is "what do the data mean for how to improve our program?" That is, data are read and given meaning for advice giving. It is in this hermeneutic, this reading of data for use, that is seen how both evaluation and applied sociobehavioral and interpretative sciences can be used for advice giving that can be practical, helpful, and suggestive.

This is why our introduction includes literature from the applied social and behavioral sciences, the policy sciences, and management science.

As is clear in the issue, advisory/consultation groups (EAG/ECG) have clear technical utility around evaluation credibility, legitimacy, and use of findings. These also have clear political use with constituencies (stakeholders) who want to influence how the evaluation is done and how it can (should) be used, by themselves and others. There is economic utility too in that members of evaluation advisory groups typically (we think) receive no salary (while receiving other benefits, as the text and case studies show), thus providing an evaluator with no–low-cost technical input. It is in the mix of these that the worth of an EAG/ECG shows itself. For all of these and other benefits, the use of EAG/ECG as such is not (we suspect) common practice. If so, why not?

It is the editors' hunch that the amount and type of effort necessary to organize and sustain a working, effective advisory/consultation group is beyond what some evaluators have or want to invest. It can be hard work, especially to evaluators not trained in this practice, and until now, although there have been hortatory calls for using EAGs/ECGs, there are few evaluation examples easily found and fewer guidelines easily available to evaluators. Never mind the care and feeding of evaluation, program, community, and other experts! Some of this is taken up in the text. Perhaps another plausible source of resistance to, or at least the failure to use, formal EAGs/ECGs comes from the simple fact of limited time. The groups do take time. Is the time and effort to do this work worth it?

In the abstract, the answer is unequivocally yes, especially when the evaluator is working in a new field, in a difficult space, on a complex study, on a politically contested evaluation, or the like. In a moral sense, the answer is yes, again. Good input for the evaluator should contribute to a better study, that is, one more valid, useful, credible, and legitimate than if that advice was not given or given and not used. The editors believe and think that it is at least moral to, if not immoral not to, ask for advice from insiders and outsiders, from a variety of stakeholders if, at minimum, this could make a study better, and, differently important, because it is a truism that those engaged with or participating in an evaluation tend to have a greater stake in it being done well and in using it for accountability, policy, program improvement, and other decision making, thus potentially enhancing program/service effectiveness and value. Directly related is that those affected by an evaluation have a right to be involved in that study, as a general (moral) rule. When those interested and affected can bring value to the work, it is foolish, the editors imply, not to invite their contribution. How best to do this is suggested by the case studies. Compton and Baizerman propose an EAG/ECG facilitator role, removing from the evaluator the responsibility and effort needed to ensure more effectively the solicitation, assessment, implementation, and evaluation of expert input.

It is in this and similar ways that this issue engages important concerns about technical, social, political, and cultural expertise in advice giving, and the use of evaluation advisory groups to enhance an evaluation study and the practice of evaluation. Advice asking and giving may be ordinary, everyday practices. In evaluation practice, good advice is anything but ordinary; its value sometimes is priceless.

References

Mathison, S. (2008). What is the difference between evaluation and research, and why do we care? In N. L. Smith & P. R. Brandon (Eds.), *Fundamental issues in evaluation*. New York, NY: The Guilford Press.
Patton, M. (2008). *Utilization-focused evaluation*. San Francisco, CA: Sage.

Ross VeLure Roholt
Michael L. Baizerman
Editors

ROSS VELURE ROHOLT *is an assistant professor in the School of Social Work, University of Minnesota.*

MICHAEL L. BAIZERMAN *is a professor in the School of Social Work, University of Minnesota.*

1

From Consilium to Advice: A Review of the Evaluation and Related Literature on Advisory Structures and Processes

Michael L. Baizerman, Alexander Fink, Ross VeLure Roholt

Abstract

The literature in evaluation and related disciplines on advice and advisory structures and processes is described and analyzed. The purposes of evaluation advisory groups and evaluation consultation groups are discussed, and working and formal definitions of each are provided. ©Wiley Periodicals, Inc., and the American Evaluation Association.

I n everyday evaluation practice, working evaluators seek advice from colleagues, potential and actual contractors, and from others with an interest in their specific project—including intended users, articles, and books, even friends and family. Some evaluators formalize their advice—seeking and giving advice in a group they consult more or less often over a short to a longer term, whereas other evaluators seek counsel informally, more or less regularly.

Seeking advice from others and from texts is normative practice in all professions, presumably, although it may only be formalized in some (e.g., medicine). Professional texts in many fields exhort the use of external advice. Evaluation texts also recommend the use of advice from others for conceptualizing, conducting, and completing an evaluation, and especially

NEW DIRECTIONS FOR EVALUATION, no. 136, Winter 2012 © Wiley Periodicals, Inc., and the American Evaluation Association. Published online in Wiley Online Library (wileyonlinelibrary.com) • DOI: 10.1002/ev.20031

for enhancing the use of the evaluation and its findings for policy and program improvement (e.g., Daponte, 2008; Fitzpatrick, Sanders, & Worthen, 2011; Pankaj, Welsh, & Ostenso, 2011). Indeed, well-known models of evaluation practice advocate for the involvement of others in an evaluation so as to make more likely the effective use of the evaluation and its findings (e.g., Patton, 2008; Ryan & DeStefano, 2000).

Given the presence of the topic of advice giving in evaluation texts, articles, and reports, there is surprisingly little practical advice published on when and how to organize, manage, and utilize formal and informal evaluation consultation. This issue fills this gap. It also contributes to a beginning theorizing of advisory/consultative structure and practice. Our strategy is to introduce advice-giving and formal structures for this, present eight case studies of formal and informal structures for advice giving, and then conceptualize and theorize this practice in the categories—ethos, craft orientation, skills, and practices—in this way adding to our earlier work on evaluation capacity building (Compton, Baizerman, & Stockdill, 2002) and managing evaluation (Compton & Baizerman, 2009).

Orienting Questions

By the end of this *New Directions for Evaluation* issue, the following questions will have been addressed, and the reader should have a deeper appreciation for the subject and a firmer grasp on several approaches to organizing, managing, and utilizing an evaluation advisory group (EAG)/ evaluation consultation group (ECG). Suggestions for a training curriculum and for research on EAG/ECG complete the final chapter.

Practical Questions

- What is an evaluation advisory group/evaluation consultation group?
- What is it useful for?
- How can it contribute to better and/or more useful evaluations?
- What are the basic structures of an evaluation advisory group/evaluation consultation group?
- How is an EAG/ECG constructed?
- How does it operate?
- How can it be managed?
- Can it be evaluated?
- What are formats for requesting advice and counsel?
- How does one assess and decide whether to use EAG advice?
- What is the timing for requesting advice?
- What are some ways to use EAG/ECG for policy making and program improvement?
- What are some other uses of an EAG/ECG?
- Why should I not use an EAG/ECG?

NEW DIRECTIONS FOR EVALUATION • DOI: 10.1002/ev

Conceptual and Theoretical Questions

- What are the ethos, craft orientations, skills, and practices of EAG/ECG practice?
- What might be included in a training program for EAG practice?
- What empirical research and evaluation of EAG/ECG should be done?

Why Ask for Advice?

Simply put, advice is another person's point of view, their take on you and your situation (and you in your situation), and guidance intended to help (we presume) you think about and act in a specific situation, or more broadly and longer term. Advice can guide, it can help one get unstuck, it can teach, and can make one feel better. The Latin root of advice is *advere*, to see, hence a viewpoint (point of view). In personal relations we often seek advice from family, friends, and experts; at work we often seek out an expert first, and may also include friends and family. Why the latter two? Because they know us, and hence may know how we may not see or think about certain things (going on) and importantly because we trust them to look over/look out for our (best) interests. All of this is quite ordinary, however interpersonally complicated it may get, especially with family and friends.

When the subject or problem at hand is technical in nature, as in evaluation, it may be far more reasonable, efficient, useful, and politically and interpersonally comfortable and safe to seek counsel from experts, typically in one's own or in a nearby professional field. This can be done informally, on an ad hoc or more formal basis, once, more often, or regularly, in the short to longer term. Or one can consult and ask advice within a formal process. This formal process, along with a formal, longer-term advice-giving structure, is our focus—the evaluation advisory group/evaluation consultation group.

Whether informal or formal, advice seeking, advice giving, and advice using are practical, if at times contentious and contested ways of "getting outside" and beyond oneself to get another perspective on one's practical situation, or on a broader issue. It is also a way to gain political legitimacy and a political base for one's plan or practice, a way to find allies for proposed and ongoing actions. Such agency politics are often necessary to ensure that an evaluation can be conducted accurately, on time, and with a good chance of being used for accountability, policy, decision making, or program improvement. Politics can also take the form of perceived or actual resistance to an evaluator or to the technical aspects of their proposed or ongoing study. Agency politics are surely crucial when a major goal of an evaluation is to propose how to improve a program or an agency. It is important to remember that asking for advice is an interpersonal process, even when the advice process is formalized.

Advice is an interpersonal process, with its own politics of sex, race/ ethnicity, ideas, feelings, and status. It is cultural and social in our society to seek advice, and it is also sociocultural to wonder about one's need and want to do so, and how one who seeks counsel will be perceived by others, for example, as weak, unsure, not expert, as the wrong evaluator for the job, perhaps. In some fields, formalization of the advice process may work to marginalize such private and social concerns, yet the same formalization could also exacerbate these concerns and feelings. To ask for advice and to use it or not can show that advice can be a contested space.

Advice as such can be a contested space (VeLure Roholt & Baizerman, 2012), a place of disagreement and tension. Such disagreement can be about the substance of ideas, about style, about preference—about alternative views and ways, or about more. When advice is taken as embodied, such differences can be about more than alternative ideas and practices; advice can become personal.

Formal advice structures can work to make more or less prominent the political, interpersonal, and contested aspects of the advice process. How the structure is contested, how it is given legitimacy (and of what types), how its size, member recruitment, screening, training, and representativeness; the type and frequency of meetings; and its own ways of working are some of the practical, everyday, subjects of interest when deciding whether and how to develop and use a formal advisory structure—topics we take on in the case studies and in the final chapter. Whether or not to seek advice is a relatively simple decision; to use a formal advice structure is more complicated; whether or not to seek and use advice and counsel regularly from the same set of individuals working together in a group is even more complex a decision. By the end of this text, you should be better prepared to decide for yourself, based on your context and situation.

On Advice

Advice giving and advice taking are everyday practices in personal and social life: Should I wear these shoes to match my outfit? Which MD should I see? Who has the best pizza? What horse should I bet on? Should I go out with him? What statistical test would work best for these data? How would you go about getting management on board to use the findings from our evaluation? What groups should be represented on my evaluation advisory committee? These ordinary, mundane, everyday questions in the advice domain show that *advice* is a close sibling to *opinion, suggestion,* and *recommendation* in everyday speech. This blurring of meaning in everyday use between and among advice, opinion, suggestion, and recommendation is challenged in technical language games (Wittgenstein, 1953) where an *opinion* is different from a *suggestion* and also from a *recommendation*. Each of these terms has technical meanings in different technical worlds, such as

NEW DIRECTIONS FOR EVALUATION • DOI: 10.1002/ev

social science research and evaluation, and may have yet other, different technical meanings within the social sciences and between these (psychology, anthropology, sociology, economics, political science) and evaluation.

In everyday English usage, native speakers distinguish among *advise*, *suggest*, and *recommend*. In technical/professional fields, there are clear practical and often legal differences among the three. In everyday native English, grammatical differences also obtain, with *advice* less strong an action requirement than *suggest*, and that less so than *recommend*. Each of these three terms has different Latin roots, whereas *suggestion* and *recommendation* both share *advise* in a thesaurus. *Advice* itself in its Latin origin joins *ad* (to, toward) to *videre* (to see). Advice: to see, inform, consul, tell, notify. It is also as if advice, in its foundational meaning, means "to see as I do." *Concilium* is a close relative in meaning (counsel), and is the name of the earliest formal Roman advisory structure, *Concilium Principis*, a group offering counsel to the first Roman Emperor, Augustus (Cook, 1955). Our use of the terms *advice, advisory*, and *consultation* will be conventional and follow everyday U.S. English meanings, except when we explicitly change to a technical meaning.

We use both the conventional advisory committee and consultation (consultative) committee in recognition of and deference to U.S. federal governmental usage, which tightly restricts the use of "advisory groups" (Croley & Funk, 1997; Smith, 2007).

In current evaluation texts, it is common to find advice, suggestions, and recommendations that the evaluator solicit, assess, and use informal and formal input (i.e., advice, suggestions, and recommendations) from intended users from a variety of constituencies of a particular study, colleagues, and others (e.g., Fitzpatrick, Sanders, & Worthen, 2011). Such advice can be informal, formal, or some of each, can be given by one or more persons individually and/or by persons in/as a group. This input can be more or less formally organized as an ad hoc group, a formal ongoing advisory group, or the like. The group can be called a user group, consultation group, or an advisory group.

Advice is a common word and a common, often (almost) invisible social process; it is a complex interpersonal process that can implicate one's self-conception, expertise, and vulnerability, as well as one's positional authority and one's very job. In our increasingly complex, global, fast-moving world, one often needs help from others—their perspective, insight, reflections, thoughts—what they see and think—and what they suggest—their advice. All of this ordinary advice asking and advice giving is the subject of social science research (Brown, 1955; de Leon, 1988; Maynard-Moody, 1983; Moore, 1971), as will be shown. But it is only of interest to us here when it is contextualized in a formal advice-giving structure for evaluation studies (and somewhat for evaluation policy and the managing of evaluators and an evaluation unit (Compton & Baizerman, 2009)). Yet we must remember that everyday practices very often are the same or closely similar to formal, professional practices. As Schon (1983) long ago pointed out, it is useful to distinguish "espoused theories" (or practices and skills) from "theories in use" (or practices and skills): How we talk about what we do does not necessarily map onto what we do and how we do it; as Dreyfus (2001) also shows. This means two things for us: (a) that informal, everyday advice practices can infuse, underlie, or even be the same as, formal advice practices, in part or wholly, and (b) how we talk about informal and formal advice practices may differ, whereas actual in-use practices may be similar or the same. The practical task here then is to be on the lookout for whether, to what degree, where, and how everyday advice practices turn up in formal advisory structures and practices. The literature review below illuminates some of these similarities in informal and formal advice giving, advice assessing, advice taking, and advice using.

To give this a different turn, in part we will be after "the embodied knowledge that comes only from engaging in practices in concerted co-presence with others" (Rawls, 2005, p. 5)—practices that are "things done, said, heard, felt—those recognizable" (Rawls, 2005). Put differently, how do formal evaluation advisory/consultation groups work and how does this map onto the working of everyday advice practices?

Advice practices are primordial in everyday human life; especially conjugal and group life: We ask others to help us live our lives, to make us wiser, to make those asked feel and think differently about themselves. Advice is a communicate transaction and as such is socioculturally bound to place and time. Who can be asked for advice, given who the asker is, and who can give advice of what type to which asker are socially related, everyday practices, important to us only to the extent that it reminds us that constructing a formal evaluation advisory structure means selecting members, orienting, training, and working with them, and how this is to be done with a committee may (is highly likely to) be based on practices in the larger society and culture. It is the evaluator's responsibility to attend to this.

Advice-seeking behavior can be directed at family, friends, texts, and others. Among these others are professionals chosen for their expertise, their specialized knowledge (Ericsson, 2009; Higgs & Titchen, 2001). This is simply said, but quite complicated in practice. How do we as laypersons know what is/are the relevant expertise we need/want? (by referral). How do we know if a particular other has it? (by credential). How do we assess whether the suggested expert is right for us? (by experience). All of that is pretty easy. To make it more difficult, in an evaluation context, do we want to know what school of thought the consulting evaluator subscribes to and uses? Do we want to know the exact expertise of the evaluator expert? For example, are they more qualitative than quantitative in their approach? Have they evaluated chronic disease programs before? How well does the consultant work with local physicians? Does he or she have training and/or knowledge in medical terminology?

The obvious point here is that there is expertise and there is "expertise," and it is not always easy to know or discern what this is and what one needs/wants (Briggle, 2008). This is the relevance problem. And it is not always easy to assess the appropriateness of a particular expertise to one's purpose at hand, for example, the construction and use of a formal evaluation advisory/consultation group. Here too the evaluator must take note of these distinctions in expertise. In the last chapter, we show the practical relevance of expertise assessments and decisions.

Dreyfus's five-stage model of expertise (see Compton & Baizerman, 2009) names the highest stage of expertise in Aristotle's term, as *phronesis*—wisdom, the joining of the moral and the technical. Benner, Tanner, and Chesla (1996) in nursing also make this point—the joining of the technically correct with the morally right. The evaluator who is constructing a formal evaluation consultative structure such as a group or council should attend to this distinction, especially if the evaluator intends evaluation findings to be used for policy, decision making, and program improvement—all normative (and frequently moral) choices.

We present next our formal and working definitions of evaluation advisory groups and evaluation consultation groups. These have family relationships to our definitions of evaluation capacity building (Compton et al., 2002) and managing evaluation (Compton & Baizerman, 2009).

Definitions of Evaluation Advisory Group

Evaluation advisory groups can be formally defined, but also are defined in an everyday and working sense.

Formal Definition

An evaluation consultation/advisory group is an intentionally organized and managed formal structure composed of competent and willing individual members who have agreed to proffer (offer) useful advice on how to create, conduct, and use one or more evaluation studies. By *intentionally organized and managed* is meant membership is a political appointment and may also be a substantive appointment, where members are selected on the basis of, and invited for, their technical, process, or political knowledge, and for their position in the constituency of the program being evaluated, its host organization, and/or its funder. By *competent and willing* is meant members voluntarily participate in the committee, and they can provide good advice. By *proffer useful advice* is meant members provide advice that supports a particular purpose at hand. By *create, conduct, and use* is meant that these groups are constructed by evaluators (their managers or clients) to enhance the quality of an evaluation (technical concerns), the conduct

NEW DIRECTIONS FOR EVALUATION • DOI: 10.1002/ev

of the evaluation (process concerns), and the use of evaluation findings (utilization concerns).

Everyday Definition

An evaluation consultation/advisory group is a committee or group without governing authority or responsibility that is put together and managed by an evaluator for technical advice, legitimacy, credibility, and/or prestige, and is composed of individuals with expert evaluation knowledge and experience, and may also include those with expertise and/or experience in the problem or condition being evaluated, the program, service, or its host organization, and other relevant aspects of a particular evaluation, type of evaluation, evaluation function, or evaluation unit.

Working Definition

An evaluation consultation/advisory group is a group that is based on expertise and advises an evaluator on how to best conduct evaluation and use findings. It has no governing authority, nor can it impose its advice on the evaluator who manages it.

Toward Theorizing Evaluation Consultation Advisory Groups

Evaluation consultation groups/advisory groups are structures constructed by evaluators (their managers or clients) to enhance the quality of an evaluation (technical concerns), the conduct of the evaluation (process concerns), and the use of evaluation findings (use concerns) for decision making, policy, or program improvement. Technical concerns are about scientific and methodological issues; process concerns are about the politics and practices of doing a study; and use concerns are those that join what should/can be used from an evaluation to how to best accomplish use. Use concerns are technical, processual, and political. Advisory/consultation group members may be selected for their technical, processual, and/or political knowledge, and for their position in the constituency of the program being evaluated, its host organization, its funder, or the like. Committee membership is a political appointment and may also be a substantive appointment, where the member is chosen for his or her technical evaluation competence (Stevahn, King, Ghene, & Minnema, 2005) and/or processual know-how. Members can be insiders or outsiders of the program or host organization, and those with evaluation technical competence may be more likely to be outsiders (there are very few empirical data on this). Members can be seen as supplementing the evaluator's technical competence and bringing processual and political know-how to an evaluator who is him- or herself typically an outsider to the program they are evaluating and also to its organizational home. All committee members are in some way stakeholders in the program, the host organization, the program's clients, its funders, or the evaluation itself.

Members bring these types of expertise (technical, processual, and political) to enhance the evaluation study and its use; their involvement can also serve to legitimate the study and the goal of evaluation use, and it can provide political muscle and protection for the evaluation and its use. Members may be selected because they have single or multiple types of expertise or because they represent—politically (agent of), symbolically (client or patient), or substantially (technical, processual, or political)—a constituency (stakeholder) or they possess a particular expertise. These groups are political structures as much as they are structures of expertise, and this includes the politics of expertise—different paradigms, different schools of thought, different ideas and strategies are present and to be negotiated. Types of expertise means forms of knowledge, including the technical and everyday, lay knowing, such as rules of thumb, and cookbook knowledge—the latter useful for the processual and political work of and within the committee.

Not all input by committee members meets the test of good advice. Some advice is flawed (Argyris, 2000) in that it is technically wrong or bad in terms of process or politics—that is, ineffective. Not all advice is helpful for the evaluator even when it is technically correct. Neither is all advice useful for the evaluator, in general or for a particular purpose at hand. The subject of advice giving, advice assessment, and advice taking is complex in an advisory/consultation context; the advice system can be a contested space. In this sense too, committee consultation to the evaluator is a political space, often of cross-cultural tension, if not confusion, where the cultural forms are professional expertise and lay interests. Even more complex is when the cross-cultural tensions are between or among professional expertise and lay expertise, as when the client or patient with disease and treatment experience in the program being evaluated sits on the same advisory group as physician specialists in that condition. The emergence of lay experts with lay expertise is part of a larger democratization of knowledge that has clear implications for advisory groups in several fields, including science policy (Steinbrook, 2004; Weingart, 1999) and scientific practice. Professionals no longer own and control legitimacy over technical and processual knowledge (Fischer, 2009), and they never had it over political know-how. A democratic urge is pushing advisory/consultation groups toward particular membership, and this in turn will have consequence on constructing and using evaluation advisory/consultation structures.

Theorizing EAGs/ECGs will be done more deeply in the final chapter after the case studies. Here, note only that when taken broadly, there are the interfaces between advice structure and government, and within this, between expertise and government/governing, and between professionalism and expertise and these two and governing (Fischer, 2009). This nexus of advice, expert and professional authority, and governing, that is, policy formation, decision making, program development, and improvement, covers an increasing domain in complex, active, Western scientific, and technological societies, as well as in those societies where expertise is not based in Western science or technological competence, but in religious, spiritual, or other types of expertise, including experience, age, and group membership; and including social status, as, for example, group identity, or simply, citizen. Empirically based advice may be other than scientifically proven advice in the Western sense, being also what outsiders might call indigenous expertise (see Johnston-Goodstar, 2012). In this postmodern moment (Mabry, 2002), there are many sources of knowing and expertise that are given legitimacy, credibility, prestige, authority, and power. One such is "practice knowledge" and "practice wisdom" (Higgs & Titchen, 2001). How this is contested space is presented in some of the literature reviews that follow.

Advisory groups do their work consultatively, typically (our case studies tell us) by request of the evaluator and/or a funder or the program's management. In this, advisory groups are outsiders and hence are like outside consultants advising by request of an evaluator. The literature on consulting is thus relevant to our work and is taken up in the literature review below.

Theoretically consultation, expertise/competency, professionalism, the advice system, small groups, intraorganizational politics, and evaluation practice broadly understood are some of the sources for deepening understanding of evaluation advisory/consultation structures. Almost all of this literature lives outside the evaluation field, but is easily found. Also easy to find is the limited advisory literature in evaluation, to which we turn next.

Research on Advisory Groups

There is a limited evaluation literature on EAGs/ECGs. We review this limited section first, and then review literature on advisory groups more generally from other fields. Why include a long section about advisory/consultation groups that are not for evaluation? Because there is so little written in evaluation about the theory and day-to-day practice of actually constructing and working with these structures, literature from other fields can teach these structures, how they (can) work, and how one can adapt them for evaluation use.

A review of 43 U.S. evaluation texts (see Table 1.1) primarily published since 2000 found mention in 26 (61%) to some advisory structure—a board (10, or 23%), committee (8, or 18%), group (7, or 16%), panel (2) task force (1), steering committee (1), or working group (1). When referred to, emphasis was on the value of outside advice, especially evaluation expertise, on the insights from outsiders on the program being evaluated, and on the political utility of such groups for gaining legitimacy for the evaluator study. This is sound advice, but lacks deeper philosophical, theoretical,

Table 1.1. Sources of Research on Advisory Groups

Source	Advisory Board	Advisory Committee	Advisory Group	Advisory Panel	Review Panel	Advisory Task Force	Expert Panel	Steering Committee	Working Group	No Mention
Abramson and Abramson (2008)			p. 121							
Alkin (2004)										×
Baker (2000)										×
Bamberger, Rugh, and Mabry (2011)				pp. 140, 141, 300	p. 141					
Bingham and Felbinger (2002)										×
Boulmetis and Dutwin (2005)										×
Braverman, Constantine, and Slater (2004)	p. 111									
Davidson (2005)			p. 61	p. 215						
Edwards, Scott, and Raju (2003)				p. 46						
Fink (2005)										×
Greenbaum (2000)										×
Grembowski (2001)	p. 232									
Grinnell, Gabor, and Unrau (2012)	p. 21[a]									
Guerra-Lopez (2008)										×
Hannum, Martineau, and Reinelt (2007)	p. 338	p. 484								
Hodges and Videto (2011)	pp. 9, 15, 109–110	p. 109–110								
Holden and Zimmerman (2009)							p. 14			
Kapp and Anderson (2009)	p. 124		p. 114							
Madans, Miller, Maitland, and Willis (2011)										×
McDavid and Hawthorn (2006)										×
Oermann and Gaberson (2009)										×

(Continued)

Table 1.1. (Continued)

Source	Advisory Board	Advisory Committee	Advisory Group	Advisory Panel	Review Panel	Advisory Task Force	Expert Panel	Steering Committee	Working Group	No Mention
Patton (2011a)		p. 98	p. 214							
Patton (2011b)	pp. 28, 69, 76, 78, 104[a]									
Patton (2002)										×
Patton (2008)		p. 219				p. 250				
Pirog (2009)										×
Posavac and Carey (2010)										×
Preskill and Tzavaras (2006)		pp. 57–58	p. 64		pp. 57–58			pp. 57–58	pp. 57–58	
Rossi, Lipsey, and Freeman (2004)		p. 392	p. 402							
Royse, Thyer, and Padgett (2009)	p. 337	p. 331								
Ryan and Cousins (2009)	p. 352									
Sanders (1994)										×
Smith (2010)										×
Spaulding (2008)										×
St. Leger and Schmieden (1992)										×
Stake (2004)										×
Steckler and Linnan (2002)										×
Stout, Evans, Nassim, and Raney (1997)				pp. 296, 665, 680						
Stufflebeam and Shinkfield (2007)		p. 189								
Wadsworth (1997)										×
Weinbach (2005)										×
Wholey, Hatry, and Newcomer (2010)		p. 673	pp. 39, 642							
Yarbrough, Caruthers, Shulha, and Hopson (2010)										×

[a]Phrasing searched for is mentioned, but is not necessarily relevant to evaluation advisory boards.

methodological, or political discussion about the advice system or advice structure.

Texts were found using general searches in Google Scholar, Google, Amazon.com, and the University of Minnesota library system. Publisher-specific searches were also run on major evaluation publishers: Sage Publications, Jossey-Bass, Wiley, and Lyceum Press. Book indexes and tables of contents were initially searched for the terms *advice, advisory, advisory board, advisory committee, advisory group, steering committee, committee,* and *working group.* Full text searches were made of texts available on Google Books (http://books.google.com). When such titles were available in tables of contents, texts were also searched for phrases like *stakeholder engagement, advisory board, participatory evaluation, evaluation management,* and so forth.

Few textbooks and handbooks available at the time of this survey contained any mention whatsoever of evaluation advisory boards/groups/committees. Indexes and tables of contents did not specifically mention these topics under *advisory, board, group,* or *committee.* When information was found, it was almost always identified under the topical areas *engagement of stakeholders, management of evaluation,* and sometimes *participatory/democratic evaluation.* No specific sections of any books examined thus far contain specific or substantive information about evaluation advisory boards. Characteristics of advisory boards examined seem to indicate that advisory boards are valuable, meaningful parts of many types of evaluation.

Characteristics included in one or more descriptions of evaluation advisory boards/groups/committees were:

- EABs have some to great decision-making authority over the evaluation (Braverman, Constantine, & Slater 2004, p.111).
- EABs are made up of members from a variety of backgrounds, often including and sometimes even dominated by clients of programs being evaluated (Braverman, Constantine, & Slater, 2004, p. 112).
- EABs often consider "important substantive issues, preliminary evaluation plans, draft evaluation methods or instruments, ongoing findings and results, and possible directions for policy and action" (Braverman, Constantine, & Slater, 2004, pp. 111–112; Fink, 2005, p. 19; Royse et al., 2009, p. 337; St. Leger & Schnieden, 1992, p. 17).
- EABs provide advice to evaluators on questions to ask or people to interview (Fink, 2005, p. 19; Wholey et al., 2010, p. 642).
- EABs review evaluation findings during and following the evaluation (Herman, Lyons Morris, & Taylor Fitz-Gibbon, 1978, p. 48; Wholey et al., 2010, p. 642).
- EABs make evaluation findings relevant and encourage utilization (Hannum et al., 2007, p. 338).
- EABs increase the validity of evaluation findings (Grembowski, 2001).
- EABs provide an aura of authority to evaluation findings (Rossi et al., 2004, pp. 392 and 402).

akeholders and provide stakeholder ownership and buy-in
of the evaluation and evaluation results (Hannum et al.,

a "member check" on results of evaluations (Herman
48).

provide support for internal evaluators under pressure from
organization higher-ups and can prevent evaluation from turning into
public relations (Patton, 2008, p. 219).

- EABs exist under several names, although such names do not always
indicate that the group is an EAB. Examples include Evaluation Advisory
Board, Evaluation Advisory Group, Evaluation Advisory Committee,
Evaluation Task Force, Evaluation Working Group, Evaluation Steering
Committee, Evaluation Team (Preskill & Tzavaras, 2006, pp. 57–58).

Advisory Groups in Other Fields

There is a small literature on formal advice structures in several fields.
Much of this is about law, policy, rules, and practices for organizing and
using required advisory groups (McKenzie, Neiger, & Thackeray, 2009;
National Consumer Technical Assistance Center, 2005; Smith, 2007). One
type of EAG/ECG is for citizens, typically nonexperts who "represent" the
broad public (e.g., Encyclopedia of Government Advisory Organizations,
1973). Such structures follow citizen engagement, citizen involvement, and
citizen participation requirements, and at times, demands that those who
are to be affected by a policy or program "have a voice"(Kitsap County,
2011; San Diego County, 2008). These are not directly our concern,
although attention is paid to how the advice structure is organized and, less
so, the rationale for the structure and how it is used. When organized at the
U.S. federal level, there are strict guidelines for advisory committees.

An introduction to U.S. federal guidelines for Federal Advisory Committees is spelled out in the 1972 Federal Advisory Committee Act (FACA)
(Smith, 2007). Croley and Funk (1997) review FACA and its workings. Of
likely limited interest to most evaluators, the Croley and Funk (1997) discussions of issues concerning the creation and administration of an advisory committee may be interesting, if not instructive for their practice. The
rationale for outside advice to public employees is important in the context
of a philosophy of government and the role of expertise for governmental
policy and program development, and for research focus and quality
(Fischer, 2009).

Beyond the legal guidelines about U.S. federal advisory groups, there is
interest in the public sphere about advisory groups, both citizen (Schaller,
1964) and technical. Examples of work done on the interface between advisory groups and government include Balla and Wright (2001) on Congress,
Brown (1955) on government and public advisory groups, and Preston and
Hart (1999) on the nexus between political leaders and advisory systems.

Rayner (2003) looks at expertise and democracy in public-sector decision making. Little of this work gets at the practical concerns of practicing evaluators, but it does show the deeper, more complex issues surrounding citizen participation, expertise, advisory roles, and government; some of these can inform evaluation of citizen advisory structures and processes (Krieger, 1981; Rowe & Frewer, 2000). In the technical sphere, Renn, Webler, and Wiedemann (1995) write on evaluating models for environmental discourse in citizen participation. For a British view on advisory groups to public bodies, see Anderson (1995).

A second literature, one closer to our interests, reports on scientific advisory structures. These are often studies of different types of advice structures and practices used for natural science and are typically on national or international levels. A more focused text, cited above, is by Renn et al. (1995), on environmental citizen involvement and evaluation models. At the level of the big-picture policy issues of citizen involvement and expert advisory groups is a European Commission Study (Glynn, Cunningham, & Flanagan, 2003) of scientific advisory structures and scientific advice production methodologies. This is for the government reader who wants to think broadly and widely about advisory groups and how they could be helpful. A bit closer to everyday practice is the United Kingdom's House of Commons report (2006) on scientific advice, risk, and evidence-based policy making. A political reading of U.S. scientific advisory groups is in Steinbrook (2004), showing the partisan political (mis)use of such groups. Environmental science is one such contested space. Practical, specific tool kits for advisory groups are available from the U.S. Environmental Protection Agency (2009), Superfund Community Involvement; there are also fact sheets and lessons-learned material (Axelrod, 1990). This topic gets closer to everyday issues that are in the penumbra of evaluations of family planning services and other socially contested moral issues.

A third literature is more generic and is on advisory committees in a variety of fields, academic (Houghton, 2003; Nickel, 2012), business (Clark, 1995; Clark & Fincham, 2002; Clark & Salaman, 1998), and human services (U.S. Department of Health and Human Services, 2010). The latter can be interesting because the advice givers may be clients of a social or health service. This brings these examples much closer to our interests, where it is not unusual to include employees and clients of a service or program on advisory/consultation groups.

In higher education, advisory committees are not unusual. For example, the University of Washington has a research advisory structure consisting of a Research Advisory Board, a Faculty Council on Research, and a Human Subjects Policy Board and Research Compliance and Integrity Committee. The University of Kansas Medical Center (2011) and the University of South Australia (2004) give details about advisory committee structure and practices. The medical and health domain also has a history of use of formal advisory committees.

Medical and health agencies use advisory/consultation structures for technical and stakeholder involvement (Berrow, 1993). This is true in the United States (U.S. Department of Health and Human Services, 2010) and in the United Kingdom (House of Commons, 2006), among many other countries. An example from the latter is a service users' research advisory group (Rhodes et al., 2002); another is on medical audit advisory groups (Houghton, 2003).

Moving to practical advice-giving, beyond the area of program evaluation advisory groups and across programmatic domains, a good overview of practical stories and models from the field of health planning in the United States is by the Office of the Assistant Secretary for Planning and Evaluation, U.S. Department of Health and Human Services. These reports include models and stories of community health planning advisory groups (U.S. Department of Health and Human Services, 2010). Their tool kit is clear, practical, and useful, but limited, and covers relevant topics such as the difference between a board of directors and an advisory group, "how to form an effective advisory group," and recruiting new members. An even better piece is on the website of San Diego County, California (USA) (San Diego County, 2008): "All you need to know about how to organize, plan, run, document and have a successful Advisory Committee Meeting." It includes guides and forms from a variety of organizations. Its self-evident limitation is that it is meeting focused and hence does not take up the construction of the EAG/ECG, what can/should/needs to be done between meetings, or the evaluation of the EAG/ECG. In contrast, similar examples for evaluation advisory groups are in the U.S. Centers for Disease Control and Prevention piece (Centers for Disease Control and Prevention, 2011).

Some of what is missing in the San Diego and U.S. Department of Health and Human Services examples is found in the Art Beyond Sight website (www.artbeyondsight.org/handbook/advisory-prac1.shtml), *Developing an Advisory Board: Practical Considerations*. Note the use of the word *board* instead of *committee*. This is a distinction with a difference depending on the domain of practice. The terms are interchangeable, as in this piece for nonprofits:

> Typically, the Board of Directors is the governing board for the nonprofit, responsible for hiring, firing and evaluating the . . ., identifying vision, mission, and values, setting strategic direction, and monitoring towards goal attainment in accordance with the strategic plan.

An advisory board is a committee or group without governing responsibility. They support the nonprofit's activities by providing information, resources, prestige (e.g., letterhead value), money, and so on, to the nonprofit.

This distinction also holds in business, the private sector (entrepreneur.com, *Selecting an Advisory Board: 6 Tips for Finding the Best Advisors for your Business*):

NEW DIRECTIONS FOR EVALUATION • DOI: 10.1002/ev

1. Recruit advisors for short-term objectives.
2. Advisors can help establish credibility.
3. Look for advisors in unusual places.
4. A free lunch is often better motivation than equity.
5. Don't treat advisors like employees or suppliers.
6. Set term limits.

Some of these points are easily transferable to evaluation advisory groups.

A point is made with these examples: There is much written about advisory groups in general in many fields, and much of it is good background reading and offers practical guidance for considering, organizing, working with, and, less so, evaluating an evaluation advisory/consultation committee. Although EAG/ECG practice may be undertheorized, it surely is neither underdiscussed nor underadvised. A related literature is less about advice structures as such, being focused on consultation structures and practices, especially in business (Clark, 1995). This is in the family of the advice system and its uses; it ties in experts and their presence in the consultation process (Argyris, 2000).

Consultation is an advice process in the family of the advice system: soliciting, assessing, evaluating, and using advice by outsiders and insiders on evaluation and on almost anything else. There is an analytical, critical literature in management on consultative advice (Argyris, 2000; Clark, 1995; Clark and Fincham, 2002; Clark & Salaman, 1998). Clark, alone and with colleagues, titles his work suggestively: "The Management Guru as Organizational Witch Doctor" (Clark & Salaman, 1996); "Telling Tales: Management Guru's Narratives and the Construction of Managerial Identity" (Clark & Salaman, 1998); and *Critical Consulting: New Perspectives on the Management Advice Industry* (Clark & Fincham, 2002). However, to Schein (2011), consultation is not advice, but is rather a form of helping. To Clark and Salaman (1998) it is. Together they clarify some of the issues for a more scholarly understanding of this everyday practice, the latter from sociology and the former more from psychology. Both sensitize the evaluator to the complex social, interpersonal, and psychological issues basic to understanding, providing, and using consultants. Although not specific to evaluation, questions about good versus flawed advice are significant and require evaluators' reflection, practices, and other actions. As with EAGs/ECGs, consultants can provide content, structure, and processual legitimacy, credibility, and prestige (and still be wrong!). Although not all consultants or advice givers are seen as (or aspire to be) "gurus," guru status itself may add value to the advice or work to blind the advice recipient to the truth value of the content. There are evaluation gurus: Caveat emptor! Finally note the title of the Clark and Salaman (1998) paper, with its focus on the effects on the manager of guru advice. Evaluators may want to attend to this: "I brought in—. (S)he said—, Therefore,—."

NEW DIRECTIONS FOR EVALUATION • DOI: 10.1002/ev

Advisory Groups and Expertise

Another relevant literature is on expertise in one's own and in related "communities of practice" or professions. Here, interest is in types, forms, and legitimacy of advice from the perspective of how to understand, select, screen, train, and use the expertise of advisory group members. Indeed, what is the expertise of each (potential or) actual member? Is that the expertise you want for the EAG/ECG, or might it be that you (really) want that person because of who he or she is? If EAGs/ECGs are expert advice structures, then a brief introduction to the topic of expertise could be useful.

There are enormous scholarly (Dreyfus & Dreyfus, 2004; Evans, 2008; Fischer, 2009), professional (Scarbrough, 1996), and practice (Benner et al., 1996) literatures on expert(ise) in many fields; we showed some of this in our *New Directions for Evaluation* issue on managing evaluation (Compton & Baizerman, 2009). The subject has great salience for evaluation advisory/consultation groups because one reason given for their existence and use is that members provide at least "expert advice" on conceptualizing, conducting, and using evaluation studies for accountability, decision making, policy formation, and program improvement.

On the surface, the expertise available from an EAG/ECG is about evaluation practice, broadly read, the theoretical, conceptual, and other everyday work of evaluation practice. Whoever can contribute to that may/should be solicited for advice. Does this mean only evaluators? Does it mean only professionally trained evaluators? Does it mean only evaluators professionally trained in a named evaluation education or training program? For example, is a doctorate in social work in a program that required two evaluation courses sufficient to qualify someone as an evaluator, and to accept that person's knowledge about evaluation as expert? All of this is both real and silly, and in practice far more real than silly because it is not only the advice content as such that matters with an EAG/ECG, but the legitimacy given (a) the advice giver, (b) the advice content, (c) the evaluation, (d) the EAG/ECG, (e) the evaluator, (f) their employer, and so on. There is much more here than is on the surface!

An EAG/ECG may be organized and used for other reasons beyond the purely/largely technical. A second purpose and use could be to assuage funders or other agencies; a third could be other uses such as accountability, program improvement, and policy development. How do these purposes influence what expertise is needed on the committee, and also the choice of whom to select?

An EAG/ECG is more than each advice giver or more than the set of potential advice content. It is a group to be managed (Scarbrough, 1996). There are individual members as persons and as experiences and as expertise, and there is the set of individuals who could become a social group or just a sounding board, or individuals with no pretense of groupness. As these possibilities are played out, consider too the knowledge, attitudes, skills, and needs and wants of the evaluator who will (or not) organize and work with the EAG/ECG: What ethos, craft orientation, skills, and practices might they need/want to work effectively with the EAG? What should be their expertise? Remembering the Argyris (2000), Schon (1983), and Argyris and Schon (1974) crucial distinction between espoused theories and theories in use, what are the theories in use of evaluators who work with EAGs/ECGs? The case studies and final chapter will explicate and discuss these. Remember the insight that expert practitioners, when asked about why they do as they do, often provide simple, incomplete, and even inaccurate answers because their expertise is so integral to who they are; they no longer can separate out or disaggregate the elements of their practice. Where does this leave us with regard to the evaluator and the EAG/ECG?

Applied Social Science, Policy Science, and Advice

The last relevant literature is a close relative to evaluation. Simply and incompletely put, applied social science is intended to be useful, and one form of use is providing advice (Beck, 2005; de Leon, 1988; Freeman & Rossi, 1984; Lindblom & Cohen, 1979).

During the 1980s, there were calls for social science to become more practical, that is, useful, and to become more helpful in solving social problems. Typically, this meant providing valid, useful empirical data to policy and other decision makers. Currently, the drive, the urge to engage civic and social problems and individual troubles (Mills, 1959), is named *empirically based practice*. All of this is about advice giving, whether it is the provision of data only, data and interpretation, and/or data-based suggestions or recommendations, such as policy advice (de Leon, 1988). In its aspiration, methodology, and practice, evaluation is closer to applied than theoretical social science. Mathison (2008, p. 189) frames the contrast (as) between evaluator and research this way:

- Evaluation particularizes, research generalizes.
- Evaluation is designed to improve something, while research is designed to prove something.
- Evaluation provides the basis for decision making; research provides the basis for drawing conclusions.
- Evaluation—so what? Research—what's so?
- Evaluation—how well it works? Research—how it works?
- Evaluation is about what is valuable; research is about what is.

Whether applied social science, research, or evaluation (in Mathison's view), data, whether quantitative or qualitative, are insufficient to drive advice or decisions until these are read, that is, interpreted. It is here where complications arise because interpreting data means making sense of it in a frame; that is, giving meaning is always giving meaning in/using a frame.

NEW DIRECTIONS FOR EVALUATION • DOI: 10.1002/ev

This hermeneutical process is basic to advice giving in that it works to transform information/data into a useful or practical frame—that is, make it useful. In this sense data as such are not self-evidently useful, but can be made useful for a particular purpose (at hand). Metaphor aside, data do not tell us what they mean for a particular purpose; the reader must make sense of the data and in an aesthetic, psychological, and sociopolitical sense, "make practical, usable sense." The reader can interpret the quantitative and qualitative data variously, reading it through social science or other theory or philosophy and/or through the demand of practical advice.

All of this points to philosophical (epistemological), methodological (hermeneutic), social structural (consultant–consultative organizations, formal relations, and the like), and individual issues, which frame and contextualize the use of social science and other data for practical advice giving by evaluators (and others) to government, social agencies, business, citizens, and whomever, for policy, program improvement, other decision making, accountability, and the like.

Evaluation advisory/consultation groups move into these reticula of issues when their advice is about more than what method, tool, or technique to employ in a study, and is, rather, about everything else, from how to think about the problem to using evaluation findings.

Conclusion

Where does this leave us? For the moment, and until after the case examples and discussion of these, we are left with a deeper appreciation of the advice system and a claim for why this *New Directions for Evaluation* issue is appropriate, even necessary. Advice structures and their use are not really as simple as these first appear. By the end of this issue, these structures and practices will be (more) clear and complex, as will be the practice of working with EAGs/ECGs.

References

Abramson, J., & Abramson, Z. (2008). *Survey methods in community medicine: Epidemiological research, programme evaluation, clinical trials.* London, England: John Wiley & Sons.

Alkin, M. (2004). *Evaluation roots: Tracing theorists' views and influences.* Thousand Oaks, CA: Sage.

Anderson, I. G. (1995). *Councils, committees & boards: A handbook of advisory, consultative, executive, regulatory & similar bodies in British public life.* Beckenham, England: CBD Research.

Argyris, C. (2000). *Flawed advice and the management trap.* New York, NY: Oxford University Press.

Argyris, C., & Schon, D. (1974). *Theory in practice: Increasing professional effectiveness.* San Francisco, CA: Jossey-Bass.

Axelrod, N. R. (1990). *Advisory councils.* Washington, DC: Board Source.

Baker, J. (2000). *2000.* Washington, DC: The World Bank.

Balla, S. L., & Wright, J. R. (2001). Interest groups, advisory committees, and the Congressional control of the bureaucracy. *American Journal of Political Science, 45*(4), 799–812.

Bamberger, M., Rugh, J., & Mabry, L. (2011). *RealWorld evaluation: Working under budget, time, data, and political constraints.* Thousand Oaks, CA: Sage.

Beck, U. (2005). How not to become a museum piece. *The British Journal of Sociology, 56*(3), 335–343.

Benner, P., Tanner, C. A., & Chesla, C. A. (1996). *Expertise in nursing practice: Caring, clinical judgment, and ethics.* New York, NY: Springer.

Berrow, H. D. (1993). Developing role of medical audit advisory groups. *Qualitative Health Care, 2,* 232–238.

Bingham, R., & Felbinger, C. (2002). *Evaluation in practice: A methodological approach.* New York, NY: Seven Bridges Press.

Boulmetis, J., & Dutwin, P. (2005). *The ABCs of evaluation: Timeless techniques for program and project managers.* San Francisco, CA: Jossey-Bass.

Braverman, M., Constantine, N., & Slater, J. (2004). *Foundations and evaluation: Contexts and practices for effective philanthropy.* San Francisco, CA: Jossey-Bass.

Briggle, A. (2008). Questioning expertise. *Social Studies of Science, 38*(3), 461–470.

Brown, D. S. (1955). The public advisory board as an instrument of government. *Public Administration Review, 15*(3), 196–204.

Brun, C. (2005). *A practical guide to social service evaluation.* Chicago, IL: Lyceum Books.

Centers for Disease Control and Prevention. Division of Nutrition, Physical Activity, and Obesity. (2011). *Developing and using an evaluation consultation group.* Atlanta, GA: Centers for Disease Control and Prevention.

Clark, T. (1995). *Managing consultants: Consultancy as the management of impressions.* Buckingham, England: Open University Press.

Clark, T., & Fincham, R. (Eds.). (2002). *Critical consulting: New perspectives on the management advice industry.* Malden, MA: Blackwell.

Clark, T., & Salaman, G. (1996). The management guru as organizational witchdoctor. *Organization, 3*(1), 85–107.

Clark, T., & Salaman, G. (1998). Telling tales: Management guru's narratives and the construction of managerial identity. *Journal of Management Studies, 35*(2), 137–161.

Clark, T., & Salaman, G. (2006). Creating the "right" impression: Towards a dramaturgy of management consultancy. *The Service Industries Journal, 18*(1), 18–38.

Compton, D., & Baizerman, M. (Eds.). (2009). *Managing program evaluation: Towards explicating a professional practice. New Directions for Evaluation, 121.*

Compton, D., Baizerman, M., & Stockdill, S. H. (Eds.). (2002). *The art, craft, and science of evaluation capacity building. New Directions for Evaluation, 93.*

Cook, J. (1955). *Concilium Principis: Imperial councils and counselors from Augustus to Diocletian.* Cambridge, England: Cambridge University Press.

Croley, S. P., & Funk, W. F. (1997). The federal advisory committee act and good government. *Yale Journal on Regulation, 14,* 451–485.

Daponte, B. (2008). *Evaluation essentials: Methods for conducting sound research.* San Francisco, CA: Jossey-Bass.

Davidson, E. (2005). *Evaluation methodology basics: The nuts and bolts of sound evaluation.* Thousand Oaks, CA: Sage.

de Leon, P. (1988). *Advice and consent: The development of policy sciences.* New York, NY: Russell Sage Foundation.

Dreyfus, H. (2001). *On the internet.* London, England: Routledge.

Dreyfus, H., & Dreyfus, S. (2004). The ethical implications of the five-stage skill-acquisition model. *Bulletin of Science, Technology & Sociology, 24*(3), 251–264.

Edwards, J., Scott, J., & Raju, N. (2003). *The human resources program-evaluation handbook*. Thousand Oaks, CA: Sage.

Encyclopedia of government advisory organizations. (1973). Detroit, MI: Gale Research.

Ericsson, K. (2009). *Development of professional expertise: Toward measurement of expert performance and design of optimal learning environments*. New York, NY: Cambridge University Press.

Evans, R. (2008). The sociology of expertise: The dysfunction of social fluency. *Sociology Compass*, 2(1), 281–298.

Fink, A. (2005). *Evaluation fundamentals*. Thousand Oaks, CA: Sage.

Fischer, F. (2009). *Democracy and expertise: Reorienting policy inquiry*. Oxford, England: Oxford University Press.

Fitzpatrick, J., Sanders, J., & Worthen, B. (2011). *Program evaluation: Alternative approaches and practical guidelines*. Upper Saddle River, NJ: Prentice Hall.

Freeman, H. F., & Rossi, P. H. (1984). Furthering the applied side of sociology. *American Sociological Review*, 49(4), 571–580.

Glanville, M. P. (1995). *Councils, committees, and boards: A handbook of advisory, consultative, executive, and regulatory and similar bodies in British public life*. Beckenham, England: CBD Research.

Glynn, S., Cunningham, P., & Flanagan, K. (2003). *Typifying scientific advisory structures and scientific advice production methodologies: Final report*. Prepared for Directorate-General Research, European Commission.

Greenbaum, T. (2000). *Moderating focus groups: A practical guide for group facilitation*. Thousand Oaks, CA: Sage.

Grembowski, D. (2001). *The practice of program evaluation*. Thousand Oaks, CA: Sage.

Grinnell, R., Gabor, P., & Unrau, Y. (2012). *Program evaluation for social workers: Foundations of evidence-based programs*. New York, NY: Oxford University Press.

Guerra-Lopez, I. (2008). *Performance evaluation: Proven approaches for improving programs and organizational performance*. San Francisco, CA: Jossey-Bass.

Hannum, K., Martineau, J., & Reinelt, C. (2007). *The handbook of leadership development evaluation*. San Francisco, CA: Jossey-Bass.

Herman, J. L., Lyons Morris, L., & Taylor Fitz-Gibbon, C. (1978). *Evaluator's handbook*. Newbury Park, CA: Sage Publishing.

Higgs, J., & Titchen, A. (2001). *Practice knowledge and expertise in the health professions*. Boston, MA: Butterworth-Heinemann.

Hodges, B., & Videto, D. (2011). *Assessment and planning in health programs*. Sudbury, MA: Jones & Bartlett Learning.

Holden, D., & Zimmerman, M. (2009). *A practical guide to program evaluation planning: Theory and case examples*. Thousand Oaks, CA: Sage.

Houghton, G. (2003). From audit to effectiveness: An historical evaluation of the changing role of medical audit advisory groups. *Journal of Evaluation in Clinical Practice*, 3(4), 245–253.

House of Commons, Science and Technology Committee. (2006). *Scientific advice, risk, and evidence-based policy making*. London, England: The Stationary Office. (HC9000–1).

Johnston-Goodstar, K. (2012). Decolonizing evaluation: The necessity of evaluation advisory groups in Indigenous evaluation. In R. VeLure Roholt & M. Baizerman (Eds.), *Evaluation advisory groups. New Directions for Evaluation, 136*, 109–117.

Kapp, S., & Anderson, G. (2009). *Agency-based program evaluation: Lessons from practice*. Thousand Oaks, CA: Sage.

Kitsap County, Washington. (last updated 10/5/2011). Community advisory group guidelines. Retrieved from http://www.kitsapgov.com/boards/PDF/Community%20Group%20Resources/COMMUNITY%20ADVISORY%20GROUP%20Guidelines%2010–5–11.pdf

Krieger, M. H. (1981). *Advice and planning*. Philadelphia, PA: Temple University Press.

Lindblom, C., & Cohen, D. (1979). *Usable knowledge: Social science and social problem solving*. New Haven, CT: Yale University Press.

Mabry, L. (2002). Postmodern evaluation—Or not? *American Journal of Evaluation, 23*(2), 141–157.

Madans, J., Miller, K., Maitland, A., & Willis, G. (2011). *Question evaluation methods: Contributing to the science of data quality*. Hoboken, NJ: John Wiley & Sons.

Mathison, S. (2008). What is the difference between evaluation and research, and why do we care? In N. L. Smith & P. R. Brandon (Eds.), *Fundamental issues in evaluation*. New York, NY: The Guilford Press.

Maynard-Moody, S. (1983). The usefulness of applied social science: Three views. *Policy Studies Journal, 11*(3), 528–532.

McDavid, J., & Hawthorn, L. (2006). *Program evaluation & performance measurement: An introduction to practice*. Thousand Oaks, CA: Sage.

McKenzie, J., Neiger, B., & Thackeray, R. (2009). *Planning, implementing, and evaluating health promotion programs: A primer*. San Francisco, CA: Benjamin Cummings.

Mills, C. W. (1959). *The sociological imagination*. New York, NY: Oxford Press.

Moore, M. L. (1971). The role of hostility and militancy in indigenous community health advisory groups. *American Journal of Public Health, 61*(5), 922–930.

National Consumer Technical Assistance Center. (2005). *How to develop and maintain consumer advisory boards*. Alexandria, VA: National Mental Health Association.

Nickel, P. M. (2012). *Public sociology and civic society: Governance, politics, and power*. Boulder, CO: Paradigm Publisher.

Oermann, M., & Gaberson, K. (2009). *Evaluation and testing in nursing education*. New York, NY: Spring Publishing.

Pankaj, V., Welsh, M., & Ostenso, L. (2011). Participatory analysis: Expanding stakeholder involvement in evaluation. Innovation Network. Retrieved from www.innonet.org

Patton, M. (2002). *Qualitative research & evaluation methods*. Thousand Oaks, CA: Sage.

Patton, M. (2008). *Utilization-focused evaluation*. San Francisco, CA: Sage.

Patton, M. (2011a). Developmental evaluation: Applying complexity concepts to enhance innovation and use. New York, NY: The Guilford Press.

Patton, M. (2011b). *Essentials of utilization-focused evaluation*. Thousand Oaks, CA: Sage.

Pirog, M. (2009). *Social experimentation, program evaluation, and public policy*. Hoboken, NJ: Wiley-Blackwell.

Posavac, E., & Carey, R. (2010). *Program evaluation: Methods and case studies*. Upper Saddle River, NJ: Prentice Hall.

Preskill, H., & Tzavaras, T. (2006). *Reframing evaluation through appreciative inquiry*. Thousand Oaks, CA: Sage.

Preston, T., & Hart, P. (1999). Understanding and evaluating bureaucratic politics: The nexus between political leaders and advisory systems. *Political Psychology, 20*(1), 49–98.

Rawls, A. (2005). Introduction. In H. Garfinkel, *Seeing sociologically: The routine grounds of social action* (pp. 1–98). Boulder, CO: Paradigm Publishers.

Rayner, S. (2003). Democracy in the age of assessment: Reflections on the roles of expertise and democracy in public sector decision making. *Science and Public Policy, 30*(3), 163–170.

Renn, O., Webler, T., & Wiedemann, P. (1995). *Fairness and competence in citizen participation: Evaluating models for environmental discourse*. Dordrecht, Netherlands: Kluwer Academic.

Rhodes, P., Nocon, A., Booth, M. Chowdrey, M. Y., Fabian, A., Lambert, N., Mohammed, F., & Walgrove, T. (2002). A service users research advisory group from the perspectives of both service users and researchers. *Health and Social Care in the Community, 10*(5), 402–409.

Rossi, P., Lipsey, M., & Freeman, H. (2004). *Evaluation: A systematic approach*. Thousand Oaks, CA: Sage.

Rowe, G., & Frewer, L. (2000). Public participation methods: A framework for evaluation. *Science, Technology & Human Values, 25*(1), 3–29.

Royse, D., Thyer, B., & Padgett, D. (2009). *Program evaluation: An introduction*. Belmont, CA: Wadsworth.

Ryan, K., & Cousins, J. (2009). *The SAGE international handbook of educational evaluation*. Thousand Oaks, CA: Sage.

Ryan, K. E., & DeStefano, L. (2000). Evaluation as a democratic process: promoting inclusion, dialogue, and deliberation. *New Directions for Evaluation, 85*.

San Diego County. (2008). *All you need to know about how to organize, plan, run, document and have a successful advisory committee meeting*. San Diego, CA: Author.

Sanders, J. (1994). *The program evaluation standards second edition: How to assess evaluations of educational programs*. Thousand Oaks, CA: Sage.

Scarbrough, H. (Ed.). (1996). *The management of expertise*. New York, NY: St. Martin's Press.

Schaller, L. E. (1964). Is the citizen advisory committee a threat to representative government? *Public Administration Review, 24*(3), 175–179.

Schein, E. (2011). *Helping: How to offer, give, and receive help. Understanding effective dynamics in one-to-one, group, and organizational relationships*. San Francisco, CA: Berrett-Koehler.

Schon, D. A. (1983). *The reflective practitioner: How professionals think in action*. New York, NY: Basic Books.

Smith, M. (2010). *Handbook of program evaluation for social work and health professionals*. Oxford, England: Oxford University Press.

Smith, S. (2007). *Federal advisory committees: A primer*. Washington, DC: Congressional Research Service (Order Code RL 30260).

Spaulding, D. (2008). *Program evaluation in practice: Core concepts and examples for discussion and analysis*. San Francisco, CA: Jossey-Bass.

St. Leger, A., & Schnieden, H. (1992). *Evaluating health services' effectiveness: A guide for health professionals, service managers, and policy makers*. Maidenhead, England: Open University Press.

Stake, R. (2004). *Standards-based & responsive evaluation*. Thousand Oaks, CA: Sage.

Steckler, A., & Linnan, L. (2002). *Process evaluation for public health interventions and research*. San Francisco, CA: Jossey-Bass.

Steinbrook, R. (2004). Science, politics, and federal advisory committees. *The New England Journal of Medicine, 350*(14), 1454–1460.

Stevahn, L., King, J. A., Ghene, G., & Minnema, J. (2005). Establishing essential competencies for program evaluators. *American Journal of Evaluation, 26*, 43–59.

Stout, S., Evans, A., Nassim, J., & Raney, L. (1997). *Evaluating health projects: Lessons from the literature*. Washington, DC: The World Bank.

Stufflebeam, D., & Shinkfield, A. (2007). *Evaluation theory, models, and applications*. San Francisco, CA: Jossey-Bass.

Teitel, L. (1994). *The advisory group advantage*. Retrieved from ERIC database. (ED 377782)

University of Kansas Medical Center. (2011). *Advocacy structure*. Kansas City, KS: Author.

University of South Australia. (2004). *Advocacy structures*. Retrieved from http://www.unisa.edu.au/policies/politics/academic/A38.asp

U.S. Department of Health and Human Services, Health Resources and Services Administration. (2010). *Advisory committee on interdisciplinary, community-based linkages*.

U.S. Environmental Protection Agency. (1998). *Community advisory group toolkit: For the community*. Retrieved from http://www.epa.gov/superfund/community/cag/pdfs/cagtlktc.pdf

U.S. Environmental Protection Agency. (2009). *Community advocacy groups. Community Advisory Group toolkit* (EPA 540-R.97–037). Retrieved from http://www.epa.gov /superfund/community/cag/resource.htm

VeLure Roholt, R., & Baizerman, M. (2012). Being practical, being safe: Doing evaluations in contested spaces. *Evaluation and Program Planning, 35*(1), 206–217.

Wadsworth, Y. (1997). *Everyday evaluation on the run*. St. Leonards, Australia: Allen & Unwin.

Weinbach, R. (2005). Evaluating social work services and programs. Boston, MA: Allyn & Bacon.

Weingart, P. (1999). Scientific expertise and political accountability: Paradoxes of science in politics. *Science and Public Policy, 26*(3), 151–161.

Wholey, J., Hatry, H., & Newcomer, K. (2010). *Handbook of practical program evaluation*. San Francisco, CA: Jossey-Bass.

Wittgenstein, L. (1953). *Philosophical investigations*. Oxford, England: Blackwell Publishers.

Yarbrough, D., Caruthers, F., Shulha, L., & Hopson, R. (2010). *The program evaluation standards: A guide for evaluators and evaluation users*. Thousand Oaks, CA: Sage.

MICHAEL L. BAIZERMAN *is a professor in the School of Social Work at the University of Minnesota.*

ALEXANDER FINK *is a doctoral student in the School of Social Work at the University of Minnesota.*

ROSS VELURE ROHOLT *is an assistant professor in the School of Social Work at the University of Minnesota.*

Mattessich, P. W. (2012). Advisory committees in contract and grant-funded evaluation
projects. In R. VeLure Roholt & M. L. Baizerman (Eds.), *Evaluation advisory groups. New
Directions for Evaluation, 136*, 31–48.

2

Advisory Committees in Contract and Grant-Funded Evaluation Projects

Paul W. Mattessich

Abstract

*This chapter describes the use of evaluation advisory committees in contract
and grant-funded evaluation projects. It defines what constitutes an evaluation
advisory committee. It identifies five key functions of evaluation advisory committees: stakeholder engagement, maximizing external credibility, political conciliation, promotion of methodological integrity, and promotion of use. Typical
features are explained: size, composition, meeting content, expectations for
authority, and decision making. Whether to have an advisory committee is discussed. A range of examples—from fields of human services, public health, education, and others—illustrates the uses, functions, features, and compositional
options of committees. ©Wiley Periodicals, Inc., and the American Evaluation Association.*

Advisory committees can enhance the ability of evaluators of contract
and grant-funded projects to improve scientific quality, increase the
acceptance of findings by stakeholders, and increase the amount of
use of an evaluation. However, the literature on evaluation offers only modest insight for evaluation practitioners as to how to form and manage such
committees. Patton (2008) describes evaluation "task forces" (closely synonymous with the term *advisory committee*) and indicates how they can
nurture use by intended users, but by and large, the major evaluation texts
provide no detailed advice. No studies have empirically documented the

impacts of advisory committees upon projects; nor has research offered insight regarding principles or techniques that promote effective functioning for advisory committees to strengthen an evaluation.

Evaluators have used advisory committees effectively in many projects. This chapter helps to remedy the shortage of codified, published knowledge about them, for contract and grant-funded evaluation. It provides insight for evaluators, and for those who hire evaluators, to optimize the use of advisory committees in evaluation projects.

What Is an Advisory Committee?

An advisory committee for an evaluation research project is a group of individuals, invited by the evaluator or by the evaluator's client, who jointly offer guidance, in one or more meetings, on at least one of the following: evaluation project design, data collection instruments and procedures, data analysis and interpretation, content and formats for reporting of evaluation results. As described in this article, evaluation committees can take a variety of forms, which best suit them to function effectively for a specific project within a specific context.

Key Terms

In this article, I use the following terms:

- Client: The person or organization who hires an evaluator to conduct an evaluation project. Evaluators have used terms such as sponsor (e.g., Rossi et al., 2004) or primary stakeholder (e.g., Patton, 2008). We've chosen *client* to reflect the nonacademic, practical relationships most practitioners have with the people who hire them to do evaluation work.
- Program manager: The person who manages the program on which an evaluation study will focus.
- Evaluator: The person or group hired by the client to conduct an evaluation project. The evaluator holds a position external to the organization of the client; in carrying out evaluation activities, the evaluator might stand apart from the stakeholders and staff of the program to be evaluated, or might be embedded among those stakeholders and staff.
- Evaluation: "A systematic process for an organization to obtain information on its activities, its impacts, and the effectiveness of its work, so that it can improve its activities and describe its accomplishments" (Mattessich, 2003).
- Evaluation project (or study): A time-limited effort to do evaluation of a program or policy (including design, data collection, analysis, and reporting).

Key Functions of Advisory Committees

Evaluation exists at the nexus of science and politics. It attempts to provide insight with the dual facets of scientific validity and user acceptability, two facets that are often difficult to reconcile. In addition, evaluation inherently threatens some stakeholders and other audiences. As Rossi et al. (2004, p. 374) state bluntly: "No matter how an evaluation comes out, there are some to whom the findings are good news and some to whom they are bad news."

Rossi et al. (2004) proceed to suggest that the existence of multiple stakeholders (typical of most evaluation projects) generates strain for evaluators in three main ways. First, the evaluator confronts the question of which stakeholder perspective(s) to take, or give most weight to, in designing an evaluation. Even by attempting to favor the "primary users, an evaluator might not mitigate this strain because primary users themselves may disagree on aims, questions, and uses of a study." Second, multiple stakeholders generate strain through their responses to evaluation findings. No guarantee exists that the findings will satisfy anyone. Even those who championed the research may direct their wrath toward the evaluator if a study's results fail to confirm the conclusions that those champions sought. A third strain arises in the form of communication challenges. Not all stakeholders use the same vocabulary; not all stakeholders receive information in the same way. What one group considers a profound and sound report, another might call hogwash.

Advisory committees constitute a tool for addressing the scientific and user acceptability challenges evaluators face in contract and grant-funded projects, including the three strains identified by Rossi et al. (2004). Committees can fulfill at least five functions: stakeholder engagement, maximizing external credibility, political conciliation, promotion of methodological integrity, and promotion of use. Committees fulfill these functions by contributing their expertise, connections (with stakeholders, relevant professionals, community members, etc.), and other resources throughout the design, data collection, analysis, and reporting phases of an evaluation project.

Time-limited evaluation studies, as defined earlier, constitute the frame of reference for these functions. Nonetheless, the management of internal evaluation activities (see Mattessich et al., 2009) can also leverage advisory committees to great benefit, albeit with different requirements regarding purpose and composition. In the following sections, these functions are described and examples, based on studies conducted at Wilder Research, in the fields of human services, public health, education, and others, are provided that illustrate the uses, functions, features, and structural options for such committees. (A few of these examples come from research projects other than evaluation studies, but they appear here because they provide good illustrations, which can apply to evaluation research as well as other forms of applied research.) The examples highlight how advisory committees can operate in support of an evaluation project. They also suggest

NEW DIRECTIONS FOR EVALUATION • DOI: 10.1002/ev

some ways that advisory committees, regardless of their ultimate benefits, can impede progress on a study.

For context regarding the examples, note that Wilder Research (www .wilderresearch.org) does program evaluation, conducts studies of community trends, and synthesizes existing research about effective services, to support program design, funding, and policy making in fields such as human services, education, community development, public health, and others. Wilder Research has about 100 research and technical support staff who work on 150–200 projects each year.

Stakeholder Engagement

Advisory committees offer a formal channel for stakeholder engagement, which successful evaluation projects require. Through an advisory committee, stakeholders can participate in

- Development and ongoing modification of research design, including the research questions
- Selection of data collection instruments and crafting of the process for collecting data
- Review of findings and interpretation of findings
- Review of draft reports, along with input on the format and distribution of reports

As a formal entity, an advisory committee infuses discipline into the process of stakeholder engagement. Evaluation projects rarely occur quickly. An advisory committee will keep multiple stakeholders involved throughout the course of a study. The evaluator experiences an imperative to schedule committee meetings and report to stakeholders and seek feedback on a regular basis. Stakeholders feel that imperative as well—if they fail to remain involved, the evaluator will recognize that and take appropriate action.

In addition to engaging stakeholders, an advisory committee has byproducts, which document the involvement of stakeholders. E-mails, meeting notes, attendance records, and similar items demonstrate the extent to which an evaluator attempted to, and succeeded at, engage stakeholders collectively; these items also document the extent to which individual stakeholders participated in formal meetings and other committee activities (for example, reviewing potential measurement instruments or reviewing draft reports).

Amy Leite, a Research Associate at Wilder Research, describes a developmental evaluation (see Patton, 2011; Mathison, 2005), currently in progress. In this project, the evaluators and the stakeholders have worked together on the same design team. Although the evaluators communicate with stakeholders in a variety of ways, they capitalize on the benefits of an advisory committee for substantial stakeholder engagement related to examination and analysis of evaluation findings and identification of the implications of those findings for the next steps in service system redesign.

The Community Metrics project of the East Metro Mental Health Roundtable is a long-term project to measure and report patient flow from inpatient behavioral health units to community-based services, and to assess the effectiveness of interventions to improve this flow. The advisory committee includes 8 members, including me. We have a psychiatrist from Regions Hospital, a social work supervisor from United Hospital, representatives from adult mental health from Ramsey, Dakota, and Washington Counties, a representative from adult mental health at the Minnesota Department of Health, and a representative from a community-based service provider. This project has a number of key stakeholders, but not a single client. The committee represents most of the key stakeholders of the Roundtable; we may expand the committee to include a few additional stakeholders as necessary.

The committee has added value to the project as of this point by identifying priorities for our focus. It currently is providing input to refine the design and is taking steps to gain buy-in from potential informants. We hope that the actions of the committee will ensure that results effectively reach and inform the appropriate stakeholders.

Maximizing External Credibility

External credibility refers to the perceived believability of the results of an evaluation project, to anyone outside of the circle of the evaluator and others involved in completing the project. It relates to the question: Will people, especially the primary intended users, trust the project's results? Credibility does not fall into scientific nomenclature; it is not synonymous with reliability or validity, for example.

Patton (2011, p. 314) writes, "The evaluator is also a stakeholder—not the primary stakeholder—but, *in every evaluation, an evaluator's reputation, credibility, integrity, and beliefs are on the line.* A utilization-focused evaluator is not passive in simply accepting and buying into whatever an intended user initially desires. The active–reactive–interactive–adaptive process includes an obligation on the part of the evaluator to represent the standards and principles of the profession as well as his or her own sense of morality and integrity, while also attending to and respecting the beliefs and concerns of other primary users."

An advisory committee creates a forum for transparency. Multiple individuals can observe and discuss all major decisions made by the evaluator. They can publicly challenge decisions, from whatever perspective they wish. For example, researchers and nonresearchers can question the methods for obtaining information; they can participate in the selection of specific instruments for data collection. Potential users of the evaluation findings can suggest ways to give those findings the strength they need to support decisions. Community members can describe nuances that will make the findings more relevant and credible to their constituencies; more specifically, advisory committee members who represent ethnic communities can sensitize the evaluator to nuances that can improve not only the acceptability of the evaluation findings to those communities, but the validity of the results in the eyes of all stakeholders.

Importantly, the transparency afforded by an advisory committee also demonstrates that "we've done our best." No study will ever achieve perfection. The forum created by an advisory committee sends the message that the best possible thinking went into the evaluation.

An advisory committee creates a positive reputational effect. That is, stakeholders and others who want to judge a project's credibility can look to see who participated in offering guidance to the evaluator. The individuals who judge the project's credibility include people who can affect the flow of data both into and out of the evaluation project. The names and/or organizational affiliations of advisory committee members can influence the willingness of potential suppliers of information (survey respondents, patients completing forms, staff in a program being evaluated, for example) to participate in an evaluation study. Sometimes, evaluators use this to their advantage by including the names of advisory committee members in their requests to people to participate in a study. Advisory committee members' names and affiliations, which appear on reports, for example, will also influence how readily the audiences for an evaluation project's findings accept those findings, rather than challenging or doubting them.

Different types of stakeholders will look for different types of affiliations among the members of a committee. People from varied professional sectors (e.g., business, health care, education) will look for representation from their own sectors. Community members will seek to determine if an advisory committee includes the community's voice (which, of course, can sometimes be difficult to define). People of all types, including researchers, will take note of the research professionals on an advisory committee, an assessment that will reassure them (or fail to reassure them) of the methodological quality of the work.

The combination of transparency and positive reputational effect counteracts the "inherent tension," identified by Klerman (2010), that a contracting arrangement provokes for an independent evaluation. Specifically, it lessens the likelihood that the audience for an evaluation's findings will dismiss them because of suspected bias resulting from the seller–purchaser relationship between evaluator and client.

Nicole Martin-Rogers, a Research Manager at Wilder Research, describes a health disparities study for which an advisory committee acted to increase both quality and credibility, so that the study achieved better use.

Our work on a health disparities study, at the request of the University of Minnesota School of Public Health and the Minnesota Department of Human Services, comprised one part of a project to better understand the health status and health care needs of enrollees of one of Minnesota's public health care programs. The study design included oversampling public health program enrollees who were African American, American Indian, Latino, Hmong, and Somali. The advisory committee included one individual who represented each of these communities.

This advisory group had major positive impacts in terms of advertising the study and crafting the individual invitations so that people in the community would trust it and participate. They were also very helpful and convincing when it came time to present the results of the study to the large health plans and the state.

Mattessich (2003, p. 75) summed up the importance of external credibility for those who make decisions about the development and funding of programs and policies: "Strategic management judgments about programs and policies are a blend of scientific reasoning, politics, values, and common sense. Your job is not to find the 'truth'; it is not to meet some abstract criteria of 'science'. Rather, your job is to make sure your evaluation study is *believable* to people to whom the study matters, and can withstand sincere, reasonable challenges. Your task is to make the results of your work *as credible as possible to the greatest number of relevant people.*" Advisory committees assist the evaluator to accomplish that task.

Political Conciliation

Sometimes, to achieve use, an evaluation study requires more than external credibility. The study needs one or more features that will align people who hold different, if not antagonistic, points of view, behind its findings, even if those individuals ultimately interpret and make use of the findings in different ways. The study might need to bring opposing political parties, or labor and management, for example, to accept the validity of its findings—to bring those groups to affirm, "yes, we have the facts"—even if they eventually proceed independently to develop very different routes for proceeding from those facts to action.

Kristin Dillon, a research scientist at Wilder Research, described the essential function of political conciliation that the advisory committee performed for her evaluation project:

We evaluated the Guild Incorporated Hospital-to-Home Program, which offers medical and social services to homeless people and people with chronic health conditions and serious and persistent mental illness. The program intended to decrease the use of emergency departments for nonemergency medical care, thus reducing public expenditures on health care.

Because of healthcare reform, a lot of attention recently has focused on the overuse of emergency departments. Emergency room use for non-emergency conditions costs hospitals, patients, and tax payers much money, and it creates congestion in emergency departments that prevents timely treatment of emergency conditions. A relatively small group of people with complex needs significantly overuse emergency departments. We intended to help resolve the debate over what to do about them.

The advisory committee consisted of representatives from five key agencies—the Minnesota Department of Human Services, Hearth Connection (housing nonprofit), Regions Hospital, Guild Incorporated (the nonprofit providing most services), and HealthPartners.

The committee was incredibly helpful in the development of research questions and the review of reports and external communication. The committee helped to navigate the politics of this issue in order to frame results in the most meaningful way possible.

I initially wrote a comprehensive report, as was agreed upon with the client, but the committee requested that the comprehensive report become a series of three brief reports and three accompanying one-page summaries. The first brief report focuses on the background of the program and its participants, and the second two brief reports focus on outcomes over time. The one-page summaries are geared toward key stakeholders, especially policy makers. The advisory group also strongly recommended that a vignette be added to document a personal story about one of the participants. They felt that this would help to supplement the results to appeal to a broader audience.

Most importantly, the advisory committee knew the language that needed to be used to position the reports in a neutral and credible way within the debate that is occurring. Members of the committee are well connected to key policy makers, so they have identified ways of framing information to make it more relevant to those key policy makers, including focusing on potential cost savings, aspects of the program that are easiest to replicate, and the personal stories. In addition, the members identified up front the ways in which they planned to personally use the deliverables to appeal to key stakeholders, which helped us prioritize the information we included.

Promotion of Methodological Integrity

Promotion of methodological integrity occurs in two primary ways through an advisory committee. It occurs in the form of peer review, if a committee includes research professionals. It also occurs in the form of operational improvement, as a result of input from committee members who have special knowledge of the groups expected to provide data for the evaluation project.

Peer review to promote methodological integrity. Researchers and others on the advisory committee, with various technical skills, carry out the peer-review function by recommending the latest scientific techniques, and thereby enabling the evaluator to use the most appropriate, state-of-the-art research methods. Amy Leite, a Research Associate at Wilder Research, describes the following example, which illustrates the value of technical experts who have a commitment to participating in an advisory committee and to assisting a study.

> Our project for Susan G. Komen for the Cure had an advisory committee with 13 members, including the three-person research team, three Komen staff and two Komen board members, representatives from the American Cancer Society, from the Minnesota Cancer Surveillance System, a representative from Health East Foundation, and a member representing a local nonprofit (African American Family Services). All were very active.

> The committee helped greatly, in at least two ways. The very capable epidemiologist from the Minnesota Cancer Surveillance System offered access to some relevant and very useful cancer data, which we might not have known we could access. Through her effort, we could identify a region of the state with increased risk in a more statistically sound way than we had in previous years, and certainly more so than many other states. If we had simply approached her out of context with our request, she might not have recognized how she could best meet our needs, but because she served on the committee, she understood how things fit together and what would help us. Second, each of the committee members helped to shape the data-collection methods and the key informant interview questions. We were able to pilot questions with committee members who were very knowledgeable about cancer, and also with those who were familiar with outreach/services in rural Minnesota.

Operational improvement to promote methodological integrity. Operational improvement refers to increasing the quality of research operations—the efficiency, cost, and productivity of activities to collect, analyze, and report information for an evaluation study.

Advisory committee members, especially those close to the data-collection process for a study, can assist in the identification of obstacles that might impede complete, accurate data collection. They can also offer practical tips for overcoming those obstacles. Less experienced evaluators do not always recognize the practical difficulties of data collection; even experienced evaluators require project-specific information concerning how those difficulties manifest themselves in a new situation. These difficulties include data-collection challenges related to language or literacy barriers for anyone (e.g., staff, service recipients) who must complete data-collection forms, resistance to the evaluation by anyone involved, time available for staff to complete forms, and accessibility of computers for data collection.

NEW DIRECTIONS FOR EVALUATION • DOI: 10.1002/ev

For the Issues Behind the Outcomes study, Ellen Shelton, a research scientist at Wilder Research, describes how the advisory committee not only contributed to operational improvement of the research activities, but also promoted use of the evaluation findings within the multiple ethnic and geographic communities in which service recipients resided.

> The Issues Behind the Outcomes study evaluated the experiences of four minority populations with the Minnesota Family Investment Program (the state's TANF Program). Our advisory committee had 16 members (11 from the four target populations and 5 from our research partner, the Minnesota Department of Human Services, including a Somali staff member and two DHS staff who provide liaisons to tribal communities). Professional backgrounds and affiliations of the 11 target population members were mainly in social services (related to MFIP specifically or to other social services for low-income people), but also included higher education and government. The committee helped to formulate evaluation research questions that were as credible to the target populations as to the researchers (and would therefore strengthen our ability to collect high-quality data with good cooperation in the study). The committee helped to refine research methods—for example, by helping us to resolve the question of whether the norms of some ethnic groups required different approaches to gathering data from men in contrast with women. The committee spread the word to their communities about the value and credibility of the research, thereby enhancing participation; it reviewed preliminary findings to check for cultural appropriateness of data coding and interpretation; it sorted through findings and helped to identify the most actionable recommendations.

Promotion of Use

Advisory committees promote the use of findings from an evaluation study both indirectly and directly. Evaluators plant the seeds of use starting at the beginning of every evaluation study. Appropriate research questions, high-quality methods, stakeholder engagement—these and other elements of a study influence the extent to which the primary intended users and others will likely use a study's findings. By fulfilling the four functions already described, advisory committees sow seeds of use along with the evaluator. Their work on stakeholder engagement and building external credibility, for example, indirectly leads to greater use of findings by making the study more valuable, relevant, and owned by the potential users.

Committees can also directly affect the amount and types of use of evaluation findings. They do this by consulting on formats for effective reporting; they do it by collaborating with the evaluator to develop strategies for bringing evaluation findings to all relevant audiences; they do it most actively when they participate personally in presentations and other efforts to disseminate results and interpretations. This occurred in the

Komen study and in the Issues Behind the Outcomes study, both described earlier.

> The advisory committee was instrumental in taking our key findings and working with the Komen staff and board members to develop their goals and objectives for their biannual Community Profile. I think the Komen staff found the committee to be essential in ensuring their goals and strategies align with what is happening in the larger state context. (Komen study)

> Then, when all the information from the evaluation was ready to release, advisory committee members announced to participating groups that the study was done and what the findings were. The advisory committee built public confidence that the research would benefit the communities, not just the researchers! (Issues Behind the Outcomes study)

Typical Features of Advisory Committees

Both size and composition of evaluation advisory committees are important features to consider, as well as what advisory committees focus their attention on.

Size

How many members should an advisory committee contain? No specific answer exists for that question. Based on the experience of Wilder Research, committees typically consist of 6–14 members. For any specific project, the major part of the "how many" response derives from the question of "Whom do we need to include?" discussed in the next section. Evaluators should strive to include as many members as needed to fulfill the five functions listed in the previous sections. However, remaining cognizant of principles of group dynamics, evaluators must temper their expectations lest a committee grow too large.

Composition

The evaluator, as strategist, must ask: Whom do we need to include on the advisory committee, in order to optimally enhance stakeholder engagement, external credibility, political conciliation, methodological integrity, and use? The decision requires as much art as science, as the evaluator must take into account both the positions of potential members as well as their personalities. In contract and grant-funded work, candidates for inclusion typically come from the stakeholder groups in the list below. In the terminology of Patton (2008), most, probably all, advisory group members, in every study, will represent stakeholders. Typically, only a portion of the committee will represent primary intended users.

The evaluation client. Clients commonly have representation at one or more of three levels: top-level management (usually only staff, but occasionally board), midlevel managers and program directors, and data coordinators and/or collectors. The distinctions among these three categories become more pronounced in large, complex organizations. In smaller organizations, a single person could easily fall into two or three. Top-level managers anchor the advisory committee's discussions to the overall organizational mission and strategic priorities. They ensure that recommendations from the committee will represent the organization's principal interests—broadly defined, including interests shaped by opportunities and risks external to the focal program, and perhaps not even apparent to staff who have connections solely to that program. Midlevel managers and program directors hold positions most intimately tied to planning, acquiring resources, and overseeing staff to implement activities that will produce the outputs and outcomes intended from a program or service. They offer insight in committee meetings that maximizes the likelihood that evaluation findings will have application to management decisions with tangible consequences. Data coordinators and collectors represent the voice of feasibility. One way or another, a successful evaluator must listen to that voice; however, they serve on advisory committees less often than do top and midlevel managers. This type of evaluation client representative possesses insight regarding what really must happen for sound data collection and aggregation to occur, especially in evaluation projects involving large, complex organizations where data may come through many different portals, staff, and service recipients.

Funders. Pure and simple, whoever pays for the evaluation should have the right to appoint a representative to the advisory committee. This connects the expectations of funders to the work, which increases their ownership as stakeholders (and often a primary intended user of the findings)—not to mention that it affects the likelihood of future contracts or grants from that funder to the evaluator!

Researchers and content experts. Researchers can critique methods and data sources. Content experts in a specific field can bring research knowledge and/or practice wisdom to a committee. Members of specific cultural groups can provide content knowledge of a different kind that is often unavailable to a researcher, such as understanding how the evaluation topic is likely to be perceived by study participants, how members of the group are likely to respond to requests for participation, and what critical shared cultural knowledge might remain unspoken unless specifically elicited.

Other resource controllers and regulators. Policy makers, standard-setting organizations, and similar entities will make decisions based on a study that has relevance and credibility. The likelihood that they will use a study increases if they have representation on an advisory committee.

Persons affected by program design. This group includes staff who deliver the program's services, individuals who receive service from the program, and others significantly affected by the program. Including them increases their feelings of ownership of the study, thus serving two purposes. First, it taps their wisdom for project design, data collection, analysis, and reporting. Second, it increases the likelihood that they will embrace the findings, make use of the findings, and accept changes that management might require as a result of using recommendations from the study for organizational change.

Thought leaders and critics. Some people have a lot of valuable wisdom; some people can strongly sway the opinions of others; some can cause trouble; some can play devil's advocate. Often, these people can help to round out a committee's membership, to provide benefits for the evaluator.

One more consideration regarding composition: Sometimes an evaluator will want to construct advisory committee membership in a way that the committee contains a smaller proportion of members who represent primary intended users and a larger proportion who do not represent primary intended users, or who even represent nonstakeholders. This can work to the evaluator's benefit, for example, when an evaluation client and other primary intended users don't understand the implications (research, financial, organizational, political, or other) of carrying out the work they have requested, and when the advisory committee meetings can serve to educate them. Such composition can also assist an evaluator to counter unrealistic expectations of clients and/or to reinforce the value of decisions made by the evaluator, which the client does not immediately understand. Recalling the strains identified by Rossi et al. (2004), it can help the evaluator to have a disproportionate number of non-emotionally-attached, but committed, people in the room in situations where primary intended users do not agree with one another or where certain findings might please one such user more than another.

The following example illustrates the size and composition of an advisory committee designed to work through all phases of an evaluation project and to achieve the five functions we have discussed. It contains members representing most of the groups mentioned above. The committee served The Evaluation Study of the Immediate Intervention/Underperforming Schools Program and the High Performing/Improving Schools Program of the Public Schools Accountability Act of 1999 (O'Day & Bitter, 2003, p. B-10).

American Institutes for Research, in consultation with the California Department of Education, convened an Advisory Board to provide feedback and advice on the study design, data-collection activities, and data analyses associated with this study. We met with the Advisory Board two times during each phase of the study. The Advisory Board for this project included a total of 11 representatives from: California School Boards Association; Office of the Secretary of Education; Superintendent of Washington Unified School District; Senate Education Committee; Legislative Analyst's Office; California Teachers Association; Department of Finance; Principal of Liggett Elementary in Los Angeles Unified School District; 1st grade teacher at Glenwood Elementary School in Robla School District; Assistant Superintendent of Accountability, Oakland Unified School District; Ventura County Superintendent of Schools. The first Advisory Board meeting took place on February 28, 2002, at the AIR Sacramento, CA office. During this meeting we reviewed the overall study design including the conceptual framework and construct map, the sampling techniques used for case-study site selection, and initial drafts of our data-collection instruments, including interview and focus-group protocols. The purpose of the second meeting, which took place on May 31, 2002, at the Employment Development Department office in Sacramento, CA, was to review the status of the project and the PSAA legislation, and to discuss results from preliminary student achievement data analyses and emerging themes from case-study site visits in preparation for the Phase I report. The third Advisory Board meeting was held on September 20, 2002 at the AIR office in Sacramento. The purpose of this meeting was to discuss updated information gained from site visits and achievement analyses, to discuss plans for survey administration, and to review drafts of teacher and principal surveys. The final Advisory Board meeting was held on May 9, 2003 at the AIR office in Sacramento. During this meeting we discussed results from the full set of case-study site visits, the teacher, principal, and External Evaluator surveys, and the statewide student achievement analyses in preparation for the completion of this final report.

Advisory Committee Meeting Content

There are common and most important items for advisory committees to incorporate into their agendas (and often into work outside of meetings).

Logic model development. Advisory committees frequently review and comment on program logic models, assisting the evaluator and the client to sharpen their identification of input, activities, outputs, and outcomes. In some cases, committees have the authority to finalize the models, but typically, clients decide how a logic model will represent exactly what their programs do and what outcomes they hope to achieve.

Overall design of the evaluation. Advisory committees review the evaluator's plan for an evaluation, offer comments for improvement, and assist in revising the design over the course of the project.

Identification of intended users and audiences for the evaluation. In most cases, the client has specified the intended users. However, this sometimes requires discussion, and advisory committees can assist in asking: Who primarily should use the findings from this evaluation effort? In addition, advisory committees can generate a list of other audiences who should see the information from the study. (If committee meetings result in the identification of additional users or audiences, a need may exist to invite additional members to join the committee.)

NEW DIRECTIONS FOR EVALUATION • DOI: 10.1002/ev

Facilitation of study participation. Advisory committees can help to shape the "marketing" of a study to participants (e.g., staff and service recipients who must provide data). They can also personally act to encourage participation, through written, e-mail, or verbal correspondence.

Review and interpretation of data. Advisory committees can review data as an analysis proceeds, offering insight into what the data mean and what aspects should be examined in greater detail (assuming, of course, due care taken by the evaluator to protect the confidentiality of study participants, as necessary).

Review of reports. Some or all advisory committee members can serve as an editorial review group for reports from a study. The more heterogeneous the committee, the richer will be the feedback for the evaluator, because it will embody so many different outlooks.

Presentation of information. Advisory committees can discuss and recommend the most effective vehicles for disseminating findings to stakeholders and other audiences. In some cases, advisory committee members may volunteer to present findings to individuals or groups, or to author short, descriptive pieces for distribution. This can powerfully leverage the findings, especially for studies facing higher-than-average challenges with respect to external credibility and political conciliation.

Authority/Decision-Making/Committee Obligations

The moniker *advisory committee* contains the word *advisory* for a reason. A committee does not represent the client; it does not supplant the evaluator. In almost all cases, it does not, and should not, have governance authority. Generally, the committee will provide advice that the evaluator will have the final authority to use in whatever way best suits the project.

In contract and grant-funded research, the evaluator should establish with the client (and the funder, if distinct from the client) expectations for an advisory committee, prior to extending invitations to members. (These can be amended later, if appropriate.) The client and evaluator should clarify and agree on who will make decisions about key elements of the project (major research questions, methods, etc.), and then agree on whether and how the advisory committee will add its input into those decisions. An effective approach does not require rigid, legalistic specification of parameters for behavior; it just requires adequate understanding, to avoid problems later, and specifically to avoid misleading advisory committee members about the nature of their position in the project.

Baizerman (2011) suggests that, by the end of an advisory committee's first meeting, clarity and agreement should exist on: purpose and outcomes (Why does the committee exist, and what specific goals should it achieve?); roles (Does the committee discuss, or recommend, or decide? What authority does it have?); leadership (Who convenes and facilitates the discussions?); meeting dates, times, and duration (What is each member's commitment of time?); communication structures and schedules (What will committee members see; how will they see it; and when will they see it, in relation to when they will need to discuss it?).

An Advisory Committee for Every Evaluation Project?

Do advisory committees for contract and grant-funded evaluation projects only produce benefits for an evaluator? Should an evaluator always go to the trouble of forming one? Should an evaluator ever resist a client's request to form such a committee? If so, why?

Frankly, advisory committee deliberations do not always result in beds of roses for evaluators. Committee processes involve the management of interaction among human beings. Every additional member on a committee can add a new dimension and can increase the work of the evaluator geometrically. Committee members frequently become overly enthusiastic and, without realizing the implications of their suggestions, they can attempt to turn a small study into the most significant research ever conducted. They can misunderstand the practical consequences of some decisions (with respect to methodological quality, expense, time, or other factors) and propose evaluation activities that appear simple but have absolutely no chance of succeeding.

Even the best of colleagues will not always agree with one another when they sit jointly on a committee. Moreover, by definition, effective advisory committees often require representatives from organizations or community sectors at odds with, or competing with, one another.

So, an evaluator should always diligently consider the benefits/ advantages of an advisory committee, relative to the costs/disadvantages, but after completing this informal analysis, an evaluator should usually respond in the affirmative to the question of whether to have an advisory committee. Two heads are better than one, if you will; the greater the number of perspectives, the more certain that the evaluator will do the highest-quality work and make no fatal mistakes. Most of us have seen studies, even some conducted by the largest national firms, with big price tags, that lacked credibility, and consequently resulted in no use, because the evaluators had never bothered to test their design with stakeholders, colleagues, and critics thoroughly. Advisory committees, even if they meet only once and contain only a very small number of members, provide a good insurance policy.

Another reason for a "yes" response derives from our understanding of innovation. "The computer scientist Christopher Langton observed several decades ago that innovative systems have a tendency to gravitate toward the 'edge of chaos': the fertile zone between too much order and too much anarchy" (Johnson, 2010). A good evaluator wants to create that "fertile zone." Note that, in fulfilling the five functions described earlier, an advisory committee often serves to disrupt the orderly, perhaps limited, thinking of the evaluator and to create just enough chaos to test whether the evaluation will truly produce the most informative and useful result. The committee prods the evaluator to innovate; then, through further discussion, the committee also supplies some of the tools for innovation.

What about the negatives? What costs/disadvantages might fit into the cost/benefit equation regarding use of advisory committees for contract and grant-funded projects? Time is an obvious one. The evaluator usually must allow more time for work during the design phase if members of an advisory committee will need to meet together. In addition, the evaluator will need to allow adequate time for committee members to review materials individually in preparation for meetings, or for committee members to follow up on discussions in which they offered to share ideas afterwards. Even if a committee does its work efficiently and on schedule, the time line for the design phase will most likely extend beyond the time necessary for design of a project without a committee. The evaluator needs to plan for and monitor this, within the larger time line approved for completion of a contract or grant.

However, a skilled evaluator should probably ignore the early-stage time cost because, if the evaluator uses the advisory committee well, time savings will accrue in later phases. Several of the examples provided earlier revealed, for instance, how advisory committees increased data-collection participation rates, how they improved methods to capture information more efficiently, how they added perspective so that, in the analysis phase, the evaluator would not lack crucial pieces of information. All of these consequences of effective use of an advisory committee produce time savings (not to mention higher quality work).

Notwithstanding the ability of an effective advisory committee to save time in the long run, advisory committees can certainly slow down evaluation project work in any and all phases, especially if the rules established for decision making do not enable the evaluator to take all the committee's input under advisement and to move forward with the necessary work. With respect to the health disparities study mentioned earlier, Martin-Rogers observed:

> Advisory committee members were community members with varied backgrounds, not a single type of professional, like health care providers, etc. We required that they have some familiarity with the health care system, and that they could speak English (since all advisory committee meetings took place in English). The survey instrument was developed by the committee, and it was a very tedious process that I would NOT use again or recommend. I think that process could have been completed much more quickly if we would have drafted a good first version of the survey and then gotten feedback. But the clients in this case wanted to be very democratic. The group agonized over wordsmithing every single question, which would have gone more efficiently with a first draft.

NEW DIRECTIONS FOR EVALUATION • DOI: 10.1002/ev

Conclusion

Patton (2011, p. 335) writes: "The process of engagement between the primary intended users (social innovators) and the developmental evaluator is as much the method of developmental evaluation as any particular design, methods, and data-collection tools." So it also is with advisory committees for contract and grant-funded evaluation projects. Irrespective of a study's focus, the evaluator's preferred methods, and any other features of an evaluation, advisory groups offer a mechanism for engagement with primary intended users, other stakeholders, and other individuals, in a way that increases the quality of the evaluation and heightens its potential for maximum, productive use.

Advisory committees can vary in size and composition, depending upon the needs of a project and the style of the evaluator—as long as the committee has the capability to fulfill the five functions at whatever level a project requires them. No matter what the costs, convening a committee—to enhance stakeholder engagement, external credibility, political conciliation, methodological integrity, and use—will generally prove more successful for an evaluator than attempting to accomplish those functions on his or her own.

References

Baizerman, M. (2011). *Developing and using an evaluation consultation group.* Atlanta, GA: Centers for Disease Control and Prevention, Division of Nutrition, Physical Activity, and Obesity.

Johnson, S. (2010). *Where good ideas come from: The natural history of innovation.* New York, NY: Riverhead Books.

Klerman, J. A. (2010). Contracting for independent evaluation. *Evaluation Review, 34*(4), 299–333.

Mathison, S. (Ed.). (2005). *Encyclopedia of evaluation.* Thousand Oaks, CA: Sage.

Mattessich, P. W. (2003). *The manager's guide to program evaluation.* Saint Paul, MN: Amherst H. Wilder Foundation/Fieldstone Alliance.

Mattessich, P. W., Mueller, D. P., & Holm-Hansen, C. A. (2009). Managing evaluation for program improvement at the Wilder Foundation. In D. W. Compton & M. Baizerman (Eds.), *Managing program evaluation: Towards explicating a professional practice. New Directions for Program Evaluation, 121,* 27–42.

O'Day, J., & Bitter, C. (2003). *Evaluation study of the Immediate Intervention/Underperforming Schools Program and the High Achieving/Improving Schools Program of the Public Schools Accountability Act of 1999 final report.* Sacramento, CA: American Institutes for Research.

Patton, M. Q. (2008). *Utilization-focused evaluation* (4th ed.). Thousand Oaks, CA: Sage.

Patton, M. Q. (2011). *Developmental evaluation.* New York, NY: The Guilford Press.

Rossi, P. H., Lipsey, M. W., & Freeman, H. E. (2004). *Evaluation: A systematic approach* (7th ed.). Thousand Oaks, CA: Sage.

PAUL W. MATTESSICH *is executive director of Wilder Research.*

Cohen, B. B. (2012). Advisory groups for evaluations in diverse cultural groups, communities, and contexts. In R. VeLure Roholt & M. L. Baizerman (Eds.), *Evaluation advisory
groups*. New Directions for Evaluation, 136, 49–65.

3

Advisory Groups for Evaluations in Diverse Cultural Groups, Communities, and Contexts

Barry B. Cohen

Abstract

*An advisory group constructed from within the community where a program
evaluation is conducted can be an invaluable resource to an evaluator, particularly if the evaluator is an outsider and of a different culture. The author identifies useful roles that advisory groups have played in his organization's
evaluations, and explores advisory group selection criteria, processes for identifying, vetting, and recruiting potential members who meet these criteria, and
recruitment-related pitfalls. Shortcomings of advisory groups in these contexts
are discussed. The authors examine dos, don'ts, and lessons learned from working effectively with advisory groups in diverse cultural contexts; for example,
understanding and appreciating unfamiliar styles of discourse and patterns of
interaction and how to adapt to these. Differences in age, gender, position,
social status, education, literacy, national origin, dialect, degree of assimilation,
political affiliation, clan membership, knowledge of English, and comfort with
European-American manners and customs are all at play.* ©Wiley Periodicals,
Inc., and the American Evaluation Association.

Advisory Group Roles

When doing evaluation in unfamiliar contexts and cultures, an advisory
group of community members can be an important resource, particularly if

we as evaluators are cultural outsiders. They are our experts and guides, immersed in the folkways and mores of their people, and can be wise and thoughtful about how, in culturally appropriate ways, we might address our evaluation questions in their communities. With an advisory group's support, evaluation can be a process of codiscovery in which we, one type of evaluation expert, recognize and acknowledge our standing as cultural naïfs, and, together with our advisory group, plan, design, and conduct our evaluation and then together analyze, interpret, and report our findings. At each of the following stages and steps of an evaluation study, community advisors can be invaluable support.

Engaging an advisory group in these ways also gives our evaluation local legitimacy and credibility, enhancing the likelihood of its being used by the community, as well as by the program evaluated, and by funders. These results follow from the basic contributions locals make to both how the study is shaped and how we together carry it out.

Planning and Designing the Evaluation

Advisory groups have helped us understand their community's historical and social landscapes, identifying for us its important organizations, institutions, associations, leagues, and clubs, its clan and familial structure, its formal and informal leadership and networks, as well as intracommunal patterns of cooperation, rivalry, and competition or internecine conflict. By our inviting them into a dialog about ours or the funder's evaluation questions and goals, they might also help craft the larger evaluation questions to fit their community's meanings and realities. We can then explore who they see in their community as the project's stakeholders, what interests they have in the evaluation, and how they might benefit from what is learned.

Depending on our evaluation methodology, community advisors have also helped identify data sources. This has included, for example, available documents such as community-specific directories, membership lists, and client lists from which we have drawn our samples. They have also provided us with introductions and entrée into community groups and organizations that helped us pull together focus groups—assisting us in recruiting individual constituents for ad hoc or, when appropriate, preexisting groups, providing us with space to conduct these groups, and arranging for culturally familiar refreshments and food.

Our advisory groups have also served as key informants and/or used their networks to recruit and assemble key informants from within their communities who, because of their backgrounds, experience, and positions, have enhanced our evaluation with their unique knowledge about their community and about the subjects that matter to them and us. Others are willing to talk to us openly and at length because advisory-group members have used their standing and relationship to vouch for us as people they could trust with confidential and sensitive information (Cohen, 2012). Open-ended interviews with key informants in cultural communities have provided us with rich qualitative narrative and case studies that offer deep insight into our evaluation questions from their unique community vantage.

Cultural Protocol

Advisory-group members are well positioned to inform us on the minimum essentials of respectful and appropriate attire, conduct, and discourse critical to establishing trust and rapport. These can be finely nuanced. How we greet and address and talk with people different from us in age, gender, and social status, as well as culture, will affect their willingness to talk with us and their candor in what they say.

Appropriate discourse is critical. As Western-trained social scientists working largely in European-American communities, we are schooled in the art of asking questions, in designing questionnaires and conducting interviews that are primarily interrogatories. In many societies and cultures, however, asking questions, particularly of strangers, is impolite, insulting, and confrontational. For example, in the early years of the Hmong immigration, we had prepared an interview guide framing all of our items as questions that we shared with a Hmong woman informant who would be leading a focus group for us with a group of her women peers. After she expressed concerns about asking our questions, we invited her to lead the group in her way. The subsequent transcript of the translated recording revealed that rather than asking questions, she instead had a conversation on all the topics we wanted covered. Sitting in a circle doing her own embroidery along with eight other Hmong women, she had deftly and gently guided the discussion without ever asking a question.

Even members of the same society or culture face challenges in gaining entrée. In an evaluation of a Hmong elders program we engaged as interviewers two graduate students who were second-generation Hmong women and fluent in their community's language. Before each interview the elders would vigorously inquire about their clan, grandparents, and parents to determine if there was a relationship between them and if there was, how our interviewers might appropriately address them.

Identify and Focus Evaluation Questions

Local community members, as single advisors and/or as a member of a local advisory group, can help directly with the evaluation. As we know, the evaluation process often begins when a prospective client from within a community and/or their funder contacts us about a project. We may be called or selected from among other evaluation groups on the strength of our reputation for working with their community, and, typically on its behalf. We have earned their respect and trust. They find us through word of mouth or referral from friends and associates because we had engaged

NEW DIRECTIONS FOR EVALUATION • DOI: 10.1002/ev

them or others they know as advisors or in other capacities. One practical consequence of past incorporation of local community members in our evaluation work is that they and others they know hire us, which, to our small organization, is important and validating.

As evaluators we generally begin with the client's question, then solicit input from program staff and other stakeholders as to what is at issue, what they perceive the evaluation question is, and how it can best be framed and studied. Local residents on the other hand, as those who may be or are being served by a program, often have their own opinions and advice on this. These perspectives may sometimes overlap, frequently differ, and occasionally agree. Advisory groups can help us reconcile contending interests by identifying the common ground that will satisfy the multiple and sometimes contending perspectives on what is important to know.

Outcomes and Indicators

Once framed, the evaluation questions drive our study. Our next decision is about evaluation outcomes and associated indicators. We use multiple inputs in determining these, including advice from locals who may know about the ongoing program or service by reputation, from family, friends, and neighbors who have used the program, from program staff, and from past and current program participants. As in the following example, their advice helps us define important, measurable, and practical outcomes and indicators, resulting in a more valid study, with greater legitimacy, at least among community stakeholders, and with that, greater credibility.

In an evaluation of a Hmong opiate users' aftercare program, the state agency funding the program had defined as their outcome that 20% or less of program participants would relapse, the measure of relapse being four consecutive random positive urine analyses. Program participants were largely elderly Hmong men and women. Many of the men had become addicted during their service as officers in the secret army fighting the Pathet Lao in Laos during the Vietnam War. Some were self-medicating for painful injuries and illnesses. They were now on daily methadone replacement therapy and came to the program where they participated in support groups and other activities. Program participants were relieved to participate in the program, which was in a relatively obscure and nondescript warehouse park where they could come and go without any additional stigma associated with their addiction.

Early on, we organized an advisory group of staff, participants, and a representative from the methadone program. Through translators we learned their reasons for participating in the program were different again from what the state had in mind. We asked participants why they came every day. One of the men talked about wanting to be again invited and welcomed to ceremonies and to have others come to him for advice or to borrow money. Ostracized for his addiction, he wanted to be a respected elder in his community. And one of the women talked about how she wanted her children to like her again. She had become alienated from her family after using rent and food money for drugs. She wanted her children to say she was a good mother and give her cards on her birthday. For them the question was not about relapse but about community and family reintegration that would be indicated in the ways they described. In a theory of change, family and community reintegration would be important steps to preventing relapse, as well as important qualitative indicators of recovery. We pursued these as additional outcomes and indicators.

Data-Collection Methods and Tools

Evaluation is a data-based practice, regardless of one's theoretical and actual approach. As good, practical evaluators, we need advice on how to do this best in each context and situation. Community members and program participants can proffer advice on "what around here" are data and how can it be collected, most effectively, at least cost, and the like. Being knowledgeable about their community, they can recommend ways to gather information in ways we hadn't considered.

In a study examining intergenerational patterns of alcohol, tobacco, and other drug use in Hmong, Cambodian, and Vietnamese communities we had assembled an advisory group of men and women from the respective communities, some of whom were first-generation immigrants who had been in the United States for varying lengths of time; others were second generation, having been born and educated in the United States. In developing a survey, we asked our advisory group what they considered good indicators of assimilation. A second-generation Hmong woman quickly responded that in her community, it was the extent to which fathers in households participated in domestic chores like shopping, cooking, and cleaning, and the extent to which they were involved in caring for their young children including bathing, feeding, and changing. We thought that an excellent suggestion, as did other members of the group, and created survey items that measured the level to which men were involved in these everyday household and family activities.

Engaging Community-Based Staff and Participants

Once we have questions clear, methods decided, outcomes set, data needs and wants identified, we, as evaluators, need staff to implement our study. Hiring can be a complicated decision especially for an evaluation in a local, ethnic/racial community. Advice on this from an advisory group is well sought.

In community-based evaluation we need data collectors—interviewers, translators, focus-group facilitators, observers. We often hire local residents of the identity community. Ethically, we need to recognize them for their work with a wage, honoraria, and in culturally appropriate and symbolic

NEW DIRECTIONS FOR EVALUATION • DOI: 10.1002/ev

ways that demonstrate to them and to their community our appreciation for their contributions. Advisory group members can assist in referring us to staff, community members, past clients, and other locals who can play these roles and advise us on appropriate rewards and recognition.

In our needs assessment and evaluation of the Hmong elders program mentioned above, our advisory group identified and recruited for us native Hmong speakers to serve as our focus-group facilitators and note takers. We had taken the trouble to have our interview guide translated into Hmong for them. When they arrived at our training, we learned that none of them knew how to read it, so they took it upon themselves to talk through how best to cover our items. They talked, joked, and argued through a process that took many more hours than we had planned for, but in the end, we had their buy-in for the translation they had created, practiced together, and later administered well. The information gathered across groups was fairly consistent, suggesting they had done a reliable job. We are confident based on subsequent staff feedback supporting the findings; these data were valid because of their work.

We also need assistance in finding and recruiting interviewees, and here our advisory groups have been of assistance as well. In a Latino community with a high proportion of undocumented residents, our advisory group referred us to a pastor of a Latino congregation to assist in organizing an ad hoc focus group. She readily agreed. Despite the incentive of a hot meal and an honorarium, however, none of the individuals she recruited showed up, evidently fearing, after a spate of recent federal raids, that they might be identified and detained by Immigration and Customs Enforcement (ICE) agents. Another advisory group member who was a manager at a local social agency in the same neighborhood then arranged with the assistance of his programs' Spanish-speaking staff to do focus groups with program clientele who agreed to participate in lieu of their regularly scheduled activity. We trained and paid the agency's staff and interns to conduct the groups and provided honoraria to the participants, for whom we also provided refreshments.

Our advisory group members have also served as key informants or used their networks to recruit and assemble key informants from within their communities. Key informants like this have enhanced our evaluations because their backgrounds, experience, and positions give them unique knowledge, perspective, and insight about their community on matters important to them and us. Informants are willing to talk to us openly and at length because advisory group members have used their own standing and relationships to vouch for us as people they can trust with confidential and sensitive information. Open-ended interviews with key informants in cultural communities have provided us with rich qualitative narrative and case studies that offer deep insight into our evaluation questions from their unique community vantage.

NEW DIRECTIONS FOR EVALUATION • DOI: 10.1002/ev

Interpreting Evaluation Findings

Data are not self-evidently meaningful. As evaluators we make sense of these within the frame of the study as well, perhaps, within the frame of the program, the community where it's located and the population it serves. Advice here is crucial if we are to get at "what do our findings mean?" to each of these. Individuals of the population served, local residents, along with program staff and other stakeholders interested in and involved with the program, can help us see things we might have overlooked, or they may consider trivial and commonsense what may have appeared to us, as outsiders, new and important. Our practice is to invite comment from our advisory group not only to a written report but more often, in conversation about what we believe we've learned.

In our evaluation and needs assessment of a Hmong elders program we came across instances of what from our perspective was neglectful and exploitive behavior toward elders. Our interviewees, however, were reluctant to discuss this. These included instances where the sons and daughters-in-law with whom they lived would be at work for long periods of time, leaving elderly parents who didn't speak English isolated and alone or caring for grandchildren on their own. In some instances adult children were taking the elders' benefit checks. It was difficult for us to discern how extensive a problem this was because the elders were reluctant to talk about it. Staff and informants advising us on the project pointed out how this was a source of great embarrassment, reflecting negatively on their parenting. "What kind of parent am I to have raised a child who would behave in this way?" We came to understand this might be a larger issue than we were able to document.

Using Evaluation Findings

Evaluation findings are commonly used for program accountability, program improvement, policy, and decision making. Typically, this is done by management and staff of the evaluated program or service. In a community-based evaluation there may also be other stakeholder groups that want to use the findings for the same or other purposes. Who else will want to use these findings and for what purposes or ends will not always be self-evident. Having an advisory group to help sort this out—the technical, political, the cultural—is also beneficial.

For whatever purpose, the advisory group has a role to play in the dissemination of findings—helping to identify with whom we share these and planning where, when, and how to best do this, particularly within their own community. They may even agree to step up and play a role that can be very useful. Depending on the audience, a member of the advisory group can be a credible messenger sharing what's been learned in ways that will be understood and because of their respected position as, for example, a leader, an elder, or a healer will be listened to and heard. In communities

NEW DIRECTIONS FOR EVALUATION • DOI: 10.1002/ev

with an oral tradition, where many members are literate neither in their native languages nor in English, having someone speak about the findings can prove worthwhile. In situations where people are legitimately dubious about research because of past bad experiences or mistrustful of large institutions that have a history of exploiting their community or ignoring its interests, a trusted messenger can represent the findings in ways that increase the likelihood they are used.

Guidelines for Recruiting and Working With an Evaluation Advisory Group

Advisory groups we have assembled are generally comprised of diverse stakeholder groups who can provide different perspectives. In our experience five to seven members are generally sufficient. Larger groups may be unwieldy, while smaller groups may not provide sufficient breadth of knowledge, experience, and perspective. In addition small groups are not of much value if one or two key people are absent and given the inevitability of turnover, may be too unstable to provide ongoing support. Advisors are most useful when they are sufficiently well versed about the evaluation, can draw on a common knowledge base over the study's duration, and don't require repeated briefings and reminding.

Recruiting Advisory Groups

Recruiting is not without its pitfalls, but a careful and thoughtful process, though time-consuming, is a hedge against subsequent problems. After identifying the classes of stakeholders that we want to include on our advisory group (staff, clients, advocates, community residents, youth), we turn first for recommendations and referrals to reliable informants with whom we've worked in the past, to the staff of our organizational partners, and to publicly available sources, including ethnic community directories, organizational board lists and newsletters, newspaper stories, neighborhood list serves, and more. From these we can identify respected community leaders and others who are knowledgeable about the community and its culture. With the use of a snowball approach, we ask each person we contact about their availability and interest and who, in their opinion, given our purpose, would have the knowledge, experience, and/or community standing that we need. Multiple citations of the same individuals are helpful guidance in making our choice. Recruiting advisory groups in this fashion has, with a few exceptions, proved sufficient for vetting candidates.

Complexities in the recruiting process, sometimes stemming from the community's internal divisions, can prove problematic in achieving a balanced perspective, and we cannot blithely ignore these. There are differences, for example, in national origin, regional dialect, language, tribe, clan, political affiliation, level of assimilation, and level of English proficiency as

NEW DIRECTIONS FOR EVALUATION • DOI: 10.1002/ev

well as differences in gender, marital status, class, caste, status, and influence. These divisions can also entail historic rivalries or taboos prohibiting intergroup interaction, and any of these may lead to friction between participants and/or create barriers to their understanding each other and working together. In refugee communities these divisions are sometimes exacerbated by histories of civil conflict and war. Residing in the same communities are groups that not long ago in their homelands were fighting and killing one another. One colleague, for example, attended a project-related meeting at which most of the Somalis attending left when they learned the scheduled speaker was Oromo. Oromo and Somali clans in a neighboring border region became involved in violent conflicts over regional boundaries and competing territorial claims following the 1991 overthrow of regimes in their respective homelands of Ethiopia and Somalia (Adugna, 2009). Refugees from both tribes who suffered war-related trauma (Halcón et al., 2004) live in the same South Minneapolis neighborhoods.

It is not within our power to resolve these differences, but we must be aware of these when recruiting, to ensure that the members we enlist are able to offer the advice we need and seek. In extreme circumstances, depending upon the nature of our evaluation, we resort to consulting with advisors and/or informants one-on-one, rather than as a group when conditions warrant.

Attributes of Worthy Candidates

In recruiting our advisory group members, we have come to identify characteristics that distinguish between strong and weak advisory group members. Irrespective of their status or position in their community, our stronger advisory group members have been truly in touch with their communities and genuinely interested in their community's welfare. We are also interested in people who are not intimidated by the evaluation process and are willing to speak up, question, and challenge. This can sometimes be problematic when working within cultural communities with norms disapproving of open confrontation, questioning, and disagreement generally, and in particular, with people who, for reasons of age, education, or position, are treated with special respect and honor. From time to time in such situations we have private, individual conversations to avoid embarrassment or disrespect for/to those concerned.

We try to avoid overrepresentation of community residents or members who are credentialed professionals good in English but so acculturated they may not be as in touch with the average person in their community. There are also individuals that the media has identified as community spokespeople or leaders who may not have this standing within their own community. They may be of assistance, but their recognition by a dominant-culture institution as a leader or expert is no guarantee of their community bona fides. We have occasionally encountered opportunists who are trying to take advantage of the evaluation process to fulfill their personal ambitions for influence, status, and money within the dominant community. Here too they may have some needed knowledge, but their personal interests may supersede those of their own community, and, unfortunately, what they choose to tell us may be what they think we want to hear.

A final note of caution: It may happen that someone who believes he or she belongs on the advisory group is for one reason or another not invited or selected. Should such persons perceive this as a snub or slight, they could become a detractor and, if in a position of influence, could undermine or delay the evaluation, discredit the results, or just ignore these, allowing them to languish unused. We advise that anyone who wished to be included but isn't, be invited to participate in some aspect of the work, be kept abreast of project milestones as the process unfolds, and be considered an alternate in the event of member turnover.

Working With an Advisory Group

Our objective in working with an advisory group is authentic participation, engaging members for useful and meaningful advice that informs and strengthens the evaluation. Facilitating these groups requires sensitivity to group dynamics, which vary by culture, and require an appreciation on the part of the evaluator for unfamiliar styles of discourse and patterns of interaction. To these we will need to adapt for the enterprise to succeed. It takes time and patience and may not be the best approach in time-sensitive projects. In a multicultural advisory group recently observed by the author, he saw participants shudder and grimace at what he knew was an unrealistic request by the project director for members to honor on short notice. The project director, although well-meaning, was oblivious to the nonverbal cues. The group members were too polite to speak up, and didn't want to disappoint their host, but afterward had an ad hoc conversation in the parking lot. The deadline will likely come and go with little of the asked-for assistance; some members, we suspect, will find ways to excuse themselves from the project or stop attending meetings.

Serving on an advisory group may place some participants in an uncomfortable and unfamiliar role, one that may create dissonance with their traditional cultural norms. It is a difficult role to play, especially if it is contrary to a culture's rules of decorum, proper discourse, and face. Members may be deferential to the views of a respected elder or leader whom it would be inappropriate to question or contradict. Advisory group members, despite their level of involvement and commitment to the project, may also be unwilling to reveal information about sacred practices, taboo behaviors, or insider information that they believe or think is inappropriate or even dangerous to share.

In a study that was being planned and designed to examine understandings about HIV and its transmission among recent Somali immigrants, we assembled a group of primarily Somali health and human service professionals along with a couple of community leaders who were fluent in English; all were men. When asked about the prevalence of men having sex with men in their community there was a silent pause before one of the group's members spoke up. "We are Muslim men and in our tradition this is not allowed. Until we came to America we never knew such things went on." Others around the table nodded or made affirming noises of assent. At the time Somalis had the highest prevalence of HIV among all recent immigrants. In short we hit a wall touching a highly taboo subject and had to find other avenues to learning about male-on-male sex in the Somali community.

At times we have come across pseudoadvisory groups recruited and arranged by others. They may meet infrequently, and are poorly constituted and indifferently managed, with nominal if not token participation. Perhaps they were organized with good intentions, but with poor planning by evaluators with little experience in such processes. In other cases they were organized to give the appearance of a consultative and inclusive process, but their input wasn't heard or heeded. Indication of a pseudogroup is when the original participants start sending proxies or, after desultory meetings, stop attending. A few participants may stay involved but are invited only to rubber stamp the evaluator's proposals or decisions. Empty exercises like this are patronizing and demoralizing and could poison the well for the next evaluator trying to organize within the same community an authentic and viable evaluation advisory group.

In our practice, we monitor/evaluate advisory group participation (e.g., attendance) and, more importantly, whether members are contributing and participating, whether their contributions are used and/or influence decisions, and whether they ever become directly involved in any of the evaluation work. That is, do we have authentic and useful participation? Over the course of our meetings we also directly inquire about members' satisfaction with the process and their estimation of how we are doing, so that we might improve our practice or make adjustments in our composition or logistics, including, for example, meeting times and duration, locations, and so on. We are also attentive to the reliability and validity of advisor input when placed against our experience in the field. It may be necessary to add people who are more representative and/or knowledgeable than those in the initial group or to replace those who, for whatever reason, step down.

Opportunities and Threats: The Advisory Group Perspective

Advisory group members are investing freely of their time, experience, and knowledge, and they are staking their reputation and credibility but their participation in the evaluation has benefits for them. It can enhance their standing within their own community. If findings of an evaluation lead to policy changes the community supports, to additional funding for a popular program, or some other worthwhile outcome, they can take some credit for this achievement. They are also positioned to broker resources. Our hiring of interviewers or giving incentives to interviewees who they know and refer are other benefits. We have learned that even modest amounts of money to individuals in low-income, ethnic/racial communities are prized. In one project we did in the Somali community, we heard complaints from focus-group participants and facilitators our advisory group helped us recruit that "the University pays us more." Obviously it was not the first project for which some of our advisory group members had secured participants. Local businesses who supply food for community meetings or agencies and faith institutions that rent out space associated with the project also share in the resources that advisory group members can arrange.

Participation as advisory group members can also enhance their status and influence with funders and sponsors of the evaluation, reinforcing the elevation of their status as leaders, experts, or authorities with dominant-society institutions; this they can capitalize on in the future. It positions them as brokers for subsequent projects in their community and its organizations and institutions.

There are, however, risks for advisory group members in cooperating with an evaluation. We as researchers should be aware and try to avoid these. Just as engagement with a project can enhance an advisory group member's status and credibility, it can also damage it. If an evaluation design changes or a project ends prematurely, commitments they may have made about positions or incentives may go unfulfilled, causing them embarrassment. Their standing in their community can be damaged by an evaluation that results in a loss of program funding and with it community jobs and services, or in findings that cast the community in a negative light or reinforce external stereotypes.

If advisory group members reveal information about their culture and community that others in their world believe/think to be confidential, private, taboo, or sacred, this can also be troublesome for the advisory group member. Often, however, evaluators and other researchers take what they need and leave, with no apparent benefit to the community or further contact with the advisory group, failing to share what's been learned. Group members may have given a lot, but gained little, with their contributions receiving minimal recognition or acknowledgment in spite of their generous support. We go to great lengths to acknowledge their service to us and often stay in touch beyond the life of the project.

Opportunities and Challenges: The Evaluator's Perspective

The relationship between evaluator and advisory group benefits from clearly defined roles and relationships from the outset. This helps avoid problems and misunderstandings as the evaluation progresses. If the role of the group is truly advisory, this must be explicit. So too must be the group's

NEW DIRECTIONS FOR EVALUATION • DOI: 10.1002/ev

charge. All this must be worked through at the beginning of the evaluation project.

Participatory work is empowering, and over time, the group may see itself as more than advisory, wanting to make decisions and recommendations about aspects of the work outside of their role. For example, they may seek to make decisions about budget, the feasibility of one approach over another, timelines, and deliverables, all of which were in the initial proposal defining joint expectations between the funder/sponsor and the evaluator. They do not belong there!

In the end, our practice of selecting advisors and advisory groups is imperfect, and we make mistakes. We invest our trust in people who generally act in good faith, but we have had instances in which some referred individuals lacked the knowledge, connections, or experience to follow through on commitments or have overstated their ability to do so. Here is an embarrassing example. In an evaluation of a neighborhood-based crime-prevention program, we sought to assemble and conduct a focus group in the local Somali community. Our advisory group directed us to a young Somali man who, we were assured, could assemble a group through the local mosque to which he belonged. This he had done successfully for another project. We arranged for another Somali man who had reliably worked for us on other projects to translate the interview guide and facilitate the group. Arrangements were made by our intermediary to host the group at the mosque, which also agreed to prepare a Halal meal for our participants. Unfortunately when mosque leaders learned that men and women would be meeting and eating together in a mixed group they withdrew their support just a couple of hours before the group was to convene.

Our facilitator, a mature and resourceful person, arranged quickly to have the group meet at a local Somali restaurant whose owners he knew. He arranged for the space, called us, and informed us what had transpired; we readily agreed to reimburse him for all expenses. When men and women began arriving at the hastily arranged new location to which they were directed by cell phone, several of the more traditional women became upset and left, refusing to meet with unrelated male strangers in a mixed group. Though they did not participate we compensated them for their time with the promised honoraria. The group proceeded fitfully with a smaller number of participants than planned. Our putative guide had failed to take into consideration the customs, traditions, and taboos of his own community. If not for the intersession of our facilitator, who took charge of the situation, we would have lost an important opportunity and suffered yet more embarrassment with direct consequences for the evaluation and its use by the community and program for project improvement and seeking additional funding.

In another project we engaged an advisor who had a conflict of interest he did not tell us about. We had been pleased with his work with us on other projects, he had connections in the community, he was fluent and literate in several East African languages, was quite affable, and always addressed our African colleague as sister. Unknown to us, he had bid on the same project on which he was advising us. The translation he prepared of our interview guide was deliberately inaccurate. This we didn't know until the day of our focus groups. We had to cancel and reschedule these at considerable expense and worse, we had lost our client's confidence in us, which we never completely restored. Our advisor was heard to say to our client amidst the confusion of the cancellation of our two groups, "You should have hired me—I told you, they don't know what they are doing."

Such incidents have been rare exceptions. Instead earnest, committed, and thoughtful support are typical. Without this, many interesting and useful projects would have failed.

For example, on a project in the Latino community of a small Minnesota town, a local translator who was advising us reviewed our focus-group invitation. He said he'd distribute it but warned us that no one would come. The erudite Spanish of our translation would indicate to the working-class residents we hoped would attend that this wasn't meant for them. He offered to retranslate it but said we'd have better attendance if he just spread the word. He did as he promised and our focus groups were well attended.

As many of our examples suggest, as evaluators we have no corner on methodological genius or imagination. In one advisory group, a Somali member suggested we administer our survey via radio over a Somali language program with thousands of listeners, most of whom could not read Somali. In another example, our advisors to an evaluation conducted in an African American community sent us to the barbershops and hair salons to recruit focus-group participants. Another example: Advisors to a project examining why pregnant African American teens don't go for care at a local clinic recommended doing intercept interviews of pregnant teens entering and leaving a large, chain drug store.

As with all participatory methods, all of this takes a lot of time. This is so particularly when engaging with cultures outside the European American time-is-money efficiency-minded approach to life. As evaluators we have to adjust to a very different rhythm. Discussions and deliberations move at their pace. We must remember that for many, meetings are social occasions and instrumental adherence to a fixed time-driven agenda simply doesn't work, showing our outsiderness. Two-hour meetings can take 4 hours with informal conversation before and after the real work. Attendance isn't always predictable, as members deal with life's exigencies and extended family obligations. In cultures more respectful than the author's everyone gets his or her say for as long as it takes them to say it. In short, however, we find the benefits worth what for us is the wait. If we have chosen to recruit and work with a group, we patiently meet them where they are on what we call the three Ts: their time, their turf, and their terms. This is a clever aphorism, and a good guide to practice.

In projects with a short turnaround and a tight budget engaging an advisory group is probably neither practical nor worthwhile. Such projects are better suited to a traditional evaluation in which we as evaluators do it all. We would suggest, however, that depending on the evaluation questions, a project of this type in ethnic and racial communities in which we are outsiders and strangers may not yield very useful, accurate, or credible findings. In all of our evaluations there are trade-offs between methodologies and designs that are the most feasible versus those that are the most reliable and valid. Advisory groups are another tool in our tool kit to use when suited for the job at hand. How does one figure out when that is? What criteria should we use to assess this? This chapter offers some answers.

Conclusions

Engaging members of racial/ethnic communities whose members are participants in a program or clients of a service being evaluated is, in our experience, a wise, practical, and effective practice for community-based evaluations. At best, it enhances an evaluation's validity, its political and social legitimacy, and, in turn, its credibility to several audiences. And these enhance both its utility and the likelihood of its use for and by the program or service, as well as for and by the community. Their involvement as advisors is both a political and a moral act because it engages in the evaluation process those who are affected by and who most directly benefit from a good study. It is also an opportunity for nonevaluators to learn about the evaluation process, building their capacity to understand, use, and perhaps even do evaluation on their own terms in their own ways. It also creates space for their voice in how the evaluation is conducted and maybe is used. As our partners in a process of codiscovery we have much to learn from advisors and their genius and ingenuity. We are grateful for what advisors have contributed to our work, for the ongoing relationships and friendships we have with them, what we have learned from them about their and our own cultures, and how to think about and do evaluations in their communities and elsewhere where we are outsiders.

Advisory Group Takeaways

Advisory Group Roles and Responsibilities

Evaluation in racial and ethnic communities can benefit from a local advisory group's insights, knowledge, networks, and support through all aspects of the process, including, for example, framing the question, identifying outcomes and indicators, data collection and analysis, interpreting the findings, and reporting.

NEW DIRECTIONS FOR EVALUATION • DOI: 10.1002/ev

Use advisory groups within ethnic/racial communities to assist on the following evaluation tasks:

- Develop, frame, and refine the evaluation questions
- Identify community sources of data and advise on how best to collect it
- Identify and define important, practical outcomes and indicators that are meaningful to their community
- Identify, make referrals to, and help recruit community members for roles as translators, focus-group facilitators, interviewers, and observers in conducting the evaluation
- Identify prospective key informants, interviewees, and focus-group participants or community-specific directories and membership and client lists from which these can be drawn
- Identify appropriate honoraria, wages, incentives, and types of recognition
- Make sense of the data, distinguishing between the important and trivial from a community perspective
- Imagine and describe practical applications/uses of the data that would benefit their community and any related technical, political, and cultural issues this may involve
- Plan when, where, and how best to disseminate findings in their community and roles they might play in doing this as credible and trusted messengers

Advisory groups can:

- Provide the evaluation context, explaining the community's historical and social landscape
- Lend legitimacy and credibility to an evaluation and vouch for the evaluator's trustworthiness
- Explain cultural protocol including the minimum essentials for respectful and appropriate attire, conduct, and discourse in an evaluation

Seek advisory group support or insight for the following:

- Give evaluation context, explaining the community's historical and social landscape
- Provide introductions and entrée into community groups and organizations
- Explain cultural protocol, providing information on the minimum essentials of respectful and appropriate attire, conduct, and discourse
- Vouch for the evaluator's credibility, reliability, and trustworthiness

Recruiting Advisory Groups

In recruiting advisory groups use a snowball approach, asking candidates contacted to nominate others with the requisite background.

- Strong advisory group members are truly in touch with their communities and genuinely interested in their community's welfare.
- Strong advisory group members are willing to speak up, question, and challenge.
- Effective groups have five to seven members. Larger groups may be unwieldy, whereas smaller groups may not provide sufficient breadth.
- The evaluator should seek recommendations and referrals from reliable informants involved in past projects.
- Other sources to consult are publicly available, including ethnic community directories, organizational board lists and newsletters, newspaper stories, and neighborhood list serves.
- Achieve balance in recruiting by seeking representation from segments of the community whose insight and knowledge will be useful.
- Avoid overrepresentation of credentialed professionals good in English but perhaps not as in touch with average residents or members of their community.

Working With Advisory Groups

The relationship between evaluator and advisory group benefits from clearly defining roles and responsibilities. Monitor/evaluate advisor participation to determine if it is authentic and members' contributions are heard and used.

Working with advisory groups takes a lot of time and patience. In ethnic/racial communities, meet with advisors where they are at, on their time, their turf, and their terms.

In short-turnaround, tightly budgeted projects, advisory groups may not be practical or worthwhile.

References

Adugna, F. (2009). Oromo-Somali relations. Max Planck Institute for Social Anthropology. Retrieved from http://www.eth.mpg.de/cms/en/people/d/adugna/project.html

Cohen, B. B. (2012). Conducting evaluation in contested terrain: Challenges, methodology and approach in an American context. *Evaluation and Program Planning, 35*(1), 189–198.

Halcón, L. L., Robertson, C. L., Savik, K., Johnson, D. R., et al. (2004). Trauma and coping in Somali and Oromo refugee youth. *Journal of Adolescent Health, 35*(1), 17–25.

BARRY B. COHEN is executive director of Rainbow Research, Minneapolis, MN.

Compton, D. W., & Baizerman, M. L. (2012). The evolution of a philosophy and practice of evaluation advice. In R. VeLure Roholt & M. L. Baizerman (Eds.), *Evaluation advisory groups. New Directions for Evaluation, 136*, 67–76.

4

The Evolution of a Philosophy and Practice of Evaluation Advice

Donald W. Compton, Michael L. Baizerman

Abstract

Advice regarding evaluation can be solicited, given, and used in a variety of informal to formal practices, which can range from unstructured to highly structured. Gathering input into an evaluation is intended to include other perspectives and voices into a process so that the evaluation is cocreated with others to enhance its rigor, relevance, and utility. In evaluation practice, the advice system should be integrated within a model of evaluation practice and should be a component of effectively managing one or more evaluation studies. The authors draw on a combined 40-year career in evaluation and in advice giving to review their increasingly sophisticated advice-system practice. This history is mined for some real-world problems encountered and how these were addressed. Finally, the article provides suggestions on how an evaluator can include soliciting advice to create a shared understanding necessary for good evaluation practice. This we call the evaluation facilitator. ©Wiley Periodicals, Inc., and the American Evaluation Association.

The findings and conclusions in this manuscript are those of the authors and do not necessarily represent the official position of the Centers for Disease Control and Prevention.

A dvice regarding evaluations can be solicited and offered in a variety of informal to formal practices, ranging from unstructured to highly structured. We can ask friends and colleagues for their opinions and advice in passing or over lunch or at a staff meeting on the side, or a meeting can be given over fully to asking colleagues for their input. An advisory/ consultation group, committee, or council is a highly formalized, seemingly unipurpose structure for soliciting and receiving advice. (U.S. Federal law, Smith, 2007, sets strict criteria for the use of advisory groups; hence we use the words *advice* and *consultation* interchangeably.) Regardless of types and degrees of formality and organizational structure, all structures to solicit advice including evaluation advisory groups (EAGs)/evaluation consultation (consultative) groups (ECGs) have at their core a common ethos, purpose, and goal, however different their look and practices. Their goal is to solicit multiple perspectives about a study and its use.

Basic to all evaluation advice systems is the ethos (and related practices) of working together that seeks to embody a philosophy of voice in which others contribute to the evaluation. The basis of their inclusion in the advice system can be their technical knowledge or professional expertise, or they represent interests important to the evaluation such as stakeholders, or intended users and its proposed uses. Once evaluation use is introduced, it becomes clear that others are needed to give legitimacy and credibility to a study and to make use happen, that is, increase the likelihood that every study be used for accountability, decision making, policy, program improvement, conceptual clarification, and the like. We contend that formal advice systems, in our experience, are most effective when the evaluator takes on the role and practices of facilitator of the advice process, whose primary role orientation and primary interest is in soliciting, collating, synthesizing, and bringing to the group the input of the EAG/ECG members as individuals and as a collective group. Explication and illustration of this role are given in the final section.

First, we describe the evaluation advice system within our chosen models of practice, and then review our combined 40-year professional biography to show our evolving efforts to implement advice-solicitation processes as a philosophy of voice and cocreation. In the third section, we present real-world problems to which EAGs/ECGs are a reasonable approach, as well as problems caused for the evaluator and the study by various advice systems constructed and used.

Evaluation Frames

Evaluation capacity building (ECB) (Compton, Baizerman, & Stockdill, 2002) is our primary model of evaluation practice, and Patton's (2008) utilization-focused evaluation (UFE) is our primary practice frame. ECB and UFE both focus on evaluation use; UFE shows the necessity and utility of involving stakeholders and intended users throughout an evaluation. As we envision and practice advice-system work, the evaluation facilitator of the advice/consultation structure and process is carrying out a type of managing (Compton & Baizerman, 2009). Because these are well-referenced and well-known models and frames, our discussion is brief. For more in-depth descriptions, see the References section.

ECB is fully explicated in our issue of *New Directions for Evaluation* (Compton, Baizerman, & Stockdill, 2002). For our purposes, ECB is the systematic work to create ongoing structure(s) and process(es) to make evaluation and its uses regular practices in an organization's everyday ways of working. ECB is not the work on a single project; rather, it is organizational work. In our experience, Patton's (2008) utilization-focused evaluation (UFE) fits well with ECB and in turn with advisory structures, processes, and practices, because UFE includes advisory principles.

UFE is oriented to involving stakeholders and intended users in an evaluation study so as to enhance the use of evaluation findings (and other study elements) for accountability, policy-making, program improvement, and decisions. UFE, then, in our terms, is about including the voices of those who can give the evaluation credibility, while making it more likely that it will be used.

Our Professional Biography: Structuring an Evolving Philosophy of Voice

Compton has a long career in evaluation, and Baizerman has been one of his close advisors throughout. The examples are presented in Don's context. Mike came of age professionally in the 1960s and Don in the 1970s. Mike was trained in community work grounded in citizen involvement. He studied and practiced citizen organizing in New York City in the early years of the poverty program. That was formative for him. Don came to evaluation practice through sociology and education—two early sources of evaluation science—and work, finding positions as an evaluator during the field's formative years. They met and studied together in Minnesota, one of the profession's places of birth, infanthood, and later youth and maturity. This is important because evaluation practice in Minnesota emphasized the involvement of stakeholders throughout the evaluation study. Both had understanding, appreciation, and skill in small-group work, and in the intentional construction of support structures for services, programs, and later, evaluation. This formative biographical philosophy, orientations, and practices came together in how they understood the need and utility of advice/consultation.

What follows is a timeline of Don's evaluation history, what he thought, worked out, and learned about the advice system over time. Remember: In the early 1970s, when the story begins, there were no personal computers, hence no e-mail, long-distance phone calls were expensive, there was no Skype, and meetings and talk were face to face. That is, technology has had a clear, direct, and profound influence on what is advice, how it is solicited and offered, and the ease, speed, and cost of working with others on an evaluation study.

NEW DIRECTIONS FOR EVALUATION • DOI: 10.1002/ev

Preadvice/Consultation Stage (1979–1980)

Don worked as a graduate student for a renowned researcher studying young people and addiction. He was required to obtain urine samples to test whether these teenage boys had been using the substances being studied. The researcher never sought advice from the young people about this procedure and the boys had ways of showing their displeasure by eagerly and regularly making data collection difficult: A lesson learned!

Informal Advice/Consultation Stage (1981–1984): Houston Independent School District (HISD)

At HISD, evaluators generally did not seek input from anyone other than evaluation colleagues in the same unit. This was not policy; it was just the way things worked back then. It is likely that graduate-school socialization was a partial source of this, with the education bureaucracy culture of expertise another source.

Don's early evaluation work sought parents' voices on year-round schooling, involved teens in a youth poll for which they developed the questions, and sought outside advice on a study of magnet schools. His approach then was ad hoc, informal, and noncumulative.

Systematic Advice/Consultation Stage

1984–1991—Texas Education Agency (TEA). At TEA, Don worked on evaluations of special education, where he invited the statewide advocacy group to advise, and on studies of Gifted and Talented, Peer Swimming, At-Risk and Dropout programs where again he sought ad hoc, informal input. He concluded that the evaluation instruments designed for each of these could benefit from input by stakeholders, and he resolved to solicit this, seeing it both as a means to enhance evaluation validity and as his moral responsibility as an evaluator.

1991–1995—Virginia Department of Education (VDOE). Evaluation at VDOE allowed Don to broaden the evaluation system to include a variety of others who could offer insight into the programs to be evaluated and into how to best, that is, most accurately, evaluate them. These included those who were players in local or state educational policy politics, including nongovernmental organizations (professional associations, advocacy groups), state government policy and planning professionals, along with legislators, teachers, parents, and young people/students, among others. Statewide studies of at-risk youth and dropouts were enriched in this way.

Emergent here in our practice was the role of advice solicitor, a role within a larger one, evaluation facilitator. Such involvement was no longer unspoken or unusual, with, for example, Fetterman's (Fetterman & Wandersman, 2005) work on empowerment evaluation, Patton's (2008)

NEW DIRECTIONS FOR EVALUATION • DOI: 10.1002/ev

stakeholder involvement, and work in *New Directions for Evaluation* on including the voices of the marginalized and excluded, especially minorities (Madison, 1992; Ryan & DeStefano, 2000).

The facilitator role is an evaluation managing (Compton & Baizerman, 2009) strategy and is basic to the formal advice system. These facts were almost explicit, clear, and teachable by this point.

1995–2003—American Cancer Society (ACS). As the first Director, Evaluation Services, National Home Office, ACS, Don had to develop evaluation capacity (Compton et al., 2002), respond to existing demand for evaluation, and meet this on the national level, nationwide and locally/regionally. There was no dedicated budget to do evaluation studies, no trained evaluators, and few internal managers familiar with evaluation as a professional practice.

Don could not make evaluation work at a level that met AEA Standards of Practice (American Evaluation Association Guiding Principles for Evaluators, 2004), "best practices" of professional evaluation, or Don's evolved understanding of having to use internal and external advice and consultation; that is, multiple-voice inclusion had become a principle of Don's evaluator practice.

His response was the Collaborative Evaluation Fellows Project (CEFP), a joint, externally funded effort joining ACS, faculty, and graduate students at local universities' schools of public health, and local ACS offices nationwide (Mattessich, Compton, & Baizerman, 2001). More than 100 evaluations were completed. Use and useful became necessary outcomes of these studies, which, in the ACS culture, had to be practical, low-cost, completed quickly and timely, and done on a real ACS program needing evaluation input for accountability, program improvement, and/or policy refinement.

It was at ACS that our ideas about ECB (Compton et al., 2002) and managing (Compton & Baizerman, 2009) were developed in practice, and Don's explicit commitment to framing evaluation within Patton's UFE (2008) was sealed. All of these framed the advice system as a practical necessity, given the realities of programs and services, with typically multiple, contesting constituencies and their differing interests, and the Use Imperative for practical, useful evaluations. Effective use became hard to understand outside of a stakeholder and intended-users frame. This was Don's mature advice practice. Baizerman conceptualized in conversation with Don ideas about what became ECB and the development of CEFP as a practice model.

Evaluation Advice Solicitation Stage

It was at ACS and in CEFP that Don's management role and the evaluation facilitator role were developed. The latter became a leader guide to an explicit 10-step advice-system structure and detailed process. This advice system is presented in Table 4.1 in outline form.

In the CEFP context, both the 10-step structure and process worked well from a managing perspective, and were found in an external evaluation to be practical, useful, and effective. It is to us significant that beyond publishing this advice protocol—structure and process—some evaluators have not adopted this innovation (Rogers, 1962).

2001–2004—Oral Health, U.S. Centers for Disease Control and Prevention. Don was an external evaluation contractor who became the fully flourishing Evaluation Facilitator, seeking and bringing consultants and other internal and external advice givers. The evaluator's use of stakeholder input in evaluation design, implementation, data interpretation, reporting, and use was viewed by some as unnecessary.

This effort contributed to evaluation becoming institutionalized and ongoing, two criteria for ECB. Don moved from being an outside contractor to a staff position within the Office on Smoking and Health within the U.S. Centers for Disease Prevention and Control from 2004 to 2008.

Table 4.1. Overview of the 10-Step Process for a 12-Month Evaluation Study

Stage	Steps
1. Groundwork In this stage, evaluation begins when the project begins and continues throughout the process. In steps 1–3, constructing the evaluation, attention is given to how the evaluation process and findings will be used in decisions about policy and programmatic modification or termination. The construction of the study's purpose, questions, and methods are to be determined and the intended uses and users identified.	1–3 Approximately 11 weeks
2. Formalization In this stage, the formal agreements, supporting infrastructure, and details of implementation are negotiated and agreed upon. This stage includes development of the proposal and data-collection instruments and compliance with Institutional Review Board (IRB) policies.	4–5 Approximately 11 weeks
3. Implementation In this stage, the program evaluation is conducted and concluded, with preliminary analysis. Special attention is given to tentative findings and possible recommendations. In Step 8, there is greater formalization to the study's outcomes and their possible contribution; these outcomes are then reviewed by the evaluation advisory group and others.	6–8 Approximately 23 weeks
4. Utilization In this stage, the findings are translated into decisions for action.	9–10 Approximately 7 weeks

Source: Compton, Baizerman, and VeLure Roholt (2011, p. 106).

NEW DIRECTIONS FOR EVALUATION • DOI: 10.1002/ev

2008–2012—Division Nutrition, Physical Activity, and Obesity, U.S. Centers for Disease Control and Prevention. Don again was hired as a lead evaluator in a new evaluation unit, this time with an experienced evaluator as his manager. By then, he conceptualized his work as evaluation facilitator (EF), that is, making quality, timely, inclusive studies happen. All evaluations were theorized within ECB and UFE, with the EF in a managing role, and became institutionalized and ongoing.

One example was the development of a guide for state health departments on the use of Evaluation Consultation Groups (ECGs) (Baizerman, 2011). Here, the state health department's staff evaluators provided practical and conceptual input on the framing of the guide, in its examples, and in how to best make it practical and useful for themselves and their colleagues. (It was the work on that guide which led Baizerman to propose this *New Directions for Evaluation* issue).

Seen here is how a supportive manager, an EF craft perspective, authority, and permission to innovate resulted in new practices, drawing on new skills in an advice/consultation practice that was displayed on multiple levels and in multiple domains within state health departments. This is Don's mature consultation/advice practice.

This work is not without problems—practical, systemic, philosophical, theoretical, and more. Some are discussed next.

Real-World Problems

Rejection of Cocreation

Basic to any advice system is a belief that one wants/needs others to complete a project at a quality level. To reject this is to make advice/consultation irrelevant. Closely related is the second problem.

There Is Only One True View

Also basic to any advice system is a belief that there can be (and often are) alternate, contrasting, contesting views on a subject. To reject this on professional, expertise, epistemological, cultural, or other grounds renders advice/consultation irrelevant.

This is not an uncommon problem in everyday, organization-based, multiple-professional work environments. Knowledge workers, and managing them (Compton & Baizerman, 2009), can be a source of this problem, as can service providers and their clients, among others.

Use Is Unimportant

To accept that an evaluation must be practical, useful, timely, within budget, and the like seems basic to professional evaluation practice. Advice solicitation and advice giving are necessary, we argue, whether or not evaluation use is sought, if for technical issues only. Once use is introduced, advice/ consultation is available on procedural grounds and on the grounds of multiple, contested interests. Regardless of the goal of use, an advice system can be, as it were, useful.

Use of Advice/Consultation Perceived as Weakness

Some see the inclusion of an advice/consultation structure and process and practices as showing weakness, and possibly one's lack of expertise; one can be seen as vulnerable, and on this basis, subject to attack.

Evaluation Legitimacy Given By Expertise

An advice system is seen as unnecessary by those who believe that the sole necessary legitimacy of an evaluation is given by the evaluator's methodological expertise; the better the scientific method, the better (higher quality) the study, and its scientific legitimacy.

But in real-world program evaluation, there is also stakeholder contextual legitimacy. The same expertise may not also meet this test.

You Don't Have to Be (Post-) Modernist to Believe

Not only late-modernists believe that in a society there are multiple realities and meaning frames (Mabry, 2002). Yet the belief that one's point of view and one's truth are the only ones is still common in practice, if not in theory or reflection (Schön, 1983). To hold to this view is to invalidate any advice system constructed and used to gain technical, professional, or practical legitimacy for an evaluation and for evaluation practice as such.

Real-World Responses

Responding to these problems must be ongoing and regular because these issues are common and there is always some group or individual who will challenge every advice system (with the possible exception of one in which the consults are from their world—professionally, organizationally, or whatever). What are reasonable responses?

The first is necessary, basic, and often weak-seeming: Teach! Explain, explain, argue, advocate, and all the rest. It's a professional obligation to include other voices, and it is ethical practice (American Evaluation Association, 2004). Second, if you can't convince and/or have no to little management support, solicit advice anyway (!), but informally, quietly, episodically. When possible, show what is value added by the inclusion of an alternate voice. Third, invite potential and actual advice givers to ask you and your manager/administrator to be involved as voices in the next evaluation, on the grounds of validity, utility, efficiency, or the like. Context, interest, skill, and courage can help craft other responses.

Given our practice and advocacy for advice/consultation systems, finally we propose our best, experience-built and practice-tested model for realizing the ongoing, everyday invitation, inclusion, and use of multiple voices in our evaluation study and for an evaluation unit.

A Modest Proposal: Evaluation Facilitator and Best Practices

We propose an evaluation-managing role—Evaluation Facilitator (EF). It is the job of the EF to cocreate and use an appropriate study/unit-specific advice structure and process appropriate to the study (unit) at hand for the purposes of enhancing the validity and utility of a study (or unit), and its multiple legitimacies, among multiple stakeholders. All of this meets professional standards (AEA) of ethical, normative practice.

Simply put, the EF is *not* the evaluator who will conduct the study. The EF's role orientation is to ensure that the study is designed, completed, and used by its funder and other stakeholders. To that end, the EF works to bring about a *shared understanding* of the study—its purpose(s), design, implementation, and use—by its stakeholders who participate and are invited to contribute to use along the way—from conception to conceptualization, implementation, and reporting.

For best results in our work contexts and over time, shared understanding is best achieved with an orientation of EAG/ECG members to the study purpose as funded, to EAG/ECG membership roles and responsibilities, to ECB, UFE, and other relevant frames, to EAG/ECG practices and procedures, and other specifics detailed in the other case examples in this text, and in the last chapter.

All of this works best, we have found, when there is a step-by-step process, such as ours presented above; in effect, a road map. The road map works best, we found, when EAG/ECG members at the first meeting are asked to respond to draft materials, rather than to open-ended questions and other broad invitations to advise.

New technologies make EAG/ECG work much faster, less expensively, and with less intrusiveness and disruption to members, along with other efficiencies. But it simultaneously may limit the group development important to certain types of legitimacy, to use, and to the next study.

An independent facilitation of the ECG meetings should be considered. If the evaluator is a group member and not the group's facilitator, his voice is only one among many.

Conclusion

Richness is given to an evaluation study and evaluation unit by the inclusion of multiple, relevant voices—the sounds, meanings, and interests of stakeholders and relevant experts. An evaluator's practice can also be enriched by the attention, input, and the very presence of interested and involved others (stakeholders). EAG/ECG is one structural and procedural approach to both. It is a feasible, simple strategy and practice to make evaluation studies more accurate, meaningful, and consequential.

References

American Evaluation Association. (2004). *American Evaluation Association guiding principles for evaluators.* Retrieved from http://www.eval.org/Publications/Guiding Principles.asp

Baizerman, M. (2011). *Developing and using an evaluation consultation group.* Atlanta, GA: Centers for Disease Control and Prevention, Division of Nutrition, Physical Activity and Obesity.

Compton, D. W., & Baizerman, M. (Eds.). (2009). *Managing program evaluation: Towards explicating a professional orientation and practice. New Directions for Evaluation, 121.*

Compton, D., Baizerman, M., Preskill, H., Rieker, P., & Miner, K. (2001). Developing evaluation capacity while improving evaluation training in public health: The American Cancer Society's Collaborative Evaluation Fellows Project. *Evaluation and Program Planning, 24*(1), 33–40.

Compton, D., Baizerman, M., & Stockdill, S. (Eds.). (2002). *The art, craft, and science of evaluation capacity building. New Directions for Evaluation, 93.*

Compton, D. W., Baizerman, M., & VeLure Roholt, R. (2011). Managing evaluations: Responding to common problems with a 10-step process. *Canadian Journal of Program Evaluation, 25*(2), 103–123.

Fetterman, D. M., & Wandersman, A. (2005). *Empowerment evaluation principles in practice.* New York, NY: Guilford Press.

Mabry, L. (2002). Postmodern evaluation—Or not? *American Journal of Evaluation, 23*(2), 141–157.

Madison, A. (Ed.). (1992). *Minority issues in program evaluation: New Directions for Program Evaluation, 54.*

Mattessich, P., Compton, D., & Baizerman, M. (2001). What have we learned about use? Lessons from a case study. *Cancer Practice, 9* (Supplement 1), S85–91.

Patton, M. Q. (2008). *Utilization-focused evaluation* (4th ed.). Thousand Oaks, CA: Sage.

Rieker, P. (2011). *Centers for Disease Control and Prevention, Evaluation Technical Assistance Document: Division of Nutrition, Physical Activity, and Obesity (DNPAO) Partnership evaluation guidebook and resources.* Atlanta, GA: Centers for Disease Control and Prevention.

Rogers, E. M. (1962). *Diffusion of innovations.* Glencoe, IL: Free Press.

Ryan, K. E., & DeStefano, L. (2000). Evaluation as a democratic process. *Promoting inclusion, dialogue, and deliberation. New Directions for Evaluation, 85.*

Schön, D. A. (1983). *The reflective practitioner: How professionals think in action.* New York, NY: Basic Books.

Smith, S. (2007). *Federal advisory committees: A primer.* Washington, DC: Congressional Research Service.

DONALD W. COMPTON is health scientist, U.S. Centers for Disease Control, Division of Nutrition, Physical Activity, and Obesity.

MICHAEL L. BAIZERMAN is a professor in the School of Social Work, University of Minnesota.

Velure Roholt, R. (2012). Advice giving in contested space. In R. Velure Roholt &
M. Baizerman (Eds.), *Evaluation advisory groups. New Directions for Evaluation,*
136, 77–85.

5

Advice Giving in Contested Space

Ross VeLure Roholt

Abstract

Shortly after the ratification of the peace accords, the national museum of
Northern Ireland created an exhibition on the legacy of The Troubles, a term
used to refer to the previous 30 years of violent civil strife. This exhibition
aimed to address the conflicted understanding of this time period through the
inclusion of multiple stories, artifacts representing both communities, and ongo-
ing input from museum visitors. As anticipated, the exhibition was contested
even prior to its opening. An evaluator was contracted to assess visitor satisfac-
tion and learning outcomes, and provided with an evaluation advisory group
(EAG) that consisted of two high-ranking museum staff and a high-ranking
museum professional who had worked on regional and national issues for muse-
ums. This case study will describe how this EAG provided the necessary politi-
cal coverage to allow the evaluation to be designed, carried out, and used.
©Wiley Periodicals, Inc., and the American Evaluation Association.

C ontested spaces raise important questions about the entire evaluation
enterprise (VeLure Roholt & Baizerman, 2012). Much of what evaluation and evaluators take for granted in designing and doing an evaluation (e.g., neutrality, safety, stability) often are not present in contested
space. Little scholarship has focused on the theory and practice of conducting evaluations in contested spaces (Baizerman, 2012), and even less scholarship has focused on the use of evaluation advisory groups to support

evaluations and their use in such spaces. This case study describes an evaluation of a museum exhibition in Northern Ireland and how an ad hoc evaluation advisory committee worked to support the evaluator and the evaluation.

Evaluation in Contested Spaces

Northern Ireland is a contested space (Harland, 2007). It has a long history of simmering and active conflict and an entrenched and divisive political struggle. Even as active violence has receded, there remain real threats and dangers as well as a legacy of violence that pervades public life. Such a context has a direct bearing on doing and completing an evaluation study. Issues of safety, neutrality, and credibility that are taken for granted in other evaluation contexts must be intentionally addressed when doing evaluation in a contested space. The space as such challenges and raises important questions about the evaluation enterprise. For the purposes of this article, these include: Can evaluations maintain a space of neutrality? Who is best qualified to do the evaluation (an internal or external evaluator)? What attention must the evaluator give to safety—his or her own safety and that of the other evaluation stakeholders, such as interviewees and advisors/consultants? How does the evaluator role change under these conditions? Each of these questions will be engaged to describe the background and context for this case study on evaluation advice giving in Northern Ireland.

Neutrality

Very little scholarship has been directed at the issues and challenges of conducting evaluation in contested spaces (Baizerman, 2012). Patton (1997) succinctly summarizes typical advice given to beginning evaluators: "work closely with decision-makers to establish trust and support, but maintain distance to guarantee objectivity and neutrality" (p. 20). This assumption of neutrality, or even its very possibility, does not, as Smyth and Robinson (2001) show, transfer easily to violently contested spaces. There are no neutral spaces, people, or processes. Everything is political. Evaluators working in violently divided contexts must become politically sophisticated and recognize that politics and evaluation are connected (e.g., Weiss, 1993), and seen by others as intricately intertwined (VeLure Roholt & Baizerman, 2012). This is true even for external evaluators, who are often understood in the evaluation literature as being more objective and able to maintain greater levels of neutrality. This is not the case when doing evaluation in contested spaces—everyone sees everyone as having interests, everything is political, and everyone is on one side (ours) or the/an other.

External and Internal Evaluators

In violently divided contexts, the assumption that external evaluators in general have greater neutrality is challenged. External evaluators, as with external researchers, can easily be discredited as failing to understand the context, facts (on the ground), history, or legacy of violence (Smyth & Robinson, 2001). Common belief among people living in contested spaces is that outsiders have not experienced the everyday conflict and therefore cannot really know what it is like. The study may adhere to academic and professional high standards of rigor and objectivity, yet locally be seen as inaccurate, poorly done, and naïve, that is, seen as not credible by the community. This perception works to erode and lessen how evaluation findings are used.

Working with an internal evaluator often solves this problem, while creating others. First, even the perception of neutrality vanishes when the study is done by internal evaluators in these contexts. Insiders are always seen as belonging to one side or the other (Sluka, 1995; Strocka, 2008). In contested space (social) identity, what group you belong to is always attended to by community members and stakeholders (Hargie & Dickson, 2003). Regardless of whether one is an internal or external evaluator, the evaluator role and its incumbent are rarely seen as neutral. This perception raises safety concerns (VeLure Roholt & Baizerman, 2012).

Safety

When doing evaluations in a contested space, safety becomes a central concern (VeLure Roholt & Baizerman, 2012). Beginning evaluators are often not trained to attend to such safety concerns while designing, implementing, and reporting on an evaluation study. Focus is given to ethics, and maintaining confidentiality and anonymity, especially as a means of ensuring quality data collection (e.g., Worthen, Sanders, & Fitzpatrick, 1997). However, in contested spaces, evaluation can quickly become a dangerous activity for the evaluator and those who choose to participate, either as stakeholders or participants (VeLure Roholt & Baizerman, 2012).

Attending to personal safety and the safety of participants is essential not only to avoid harm but also to ensure credible and valid data collection. By attending to safety, the evaluator creates necessary conditions for participants to respond honestly. The evaluation process may need to be revised, delayed, or even halted for a period of time to ensure accurate and valid data collection and the safety of the evaluator and those participating in the evaluation study. Issues of security and safety must be addressed and attended to in addition to issues of rigor and credibility. The evaluator must be technically competent in designing and doing evaluation studies but also must be wise when deciding to begin, continue, or halt an evaluation project. The contested space as context, environment, and situation changes the nature of the evaluation enterprise, the nature of evaluation practice, and of course, the evaluator's role.

Evaluator Role

This limited review of evaluation in a contested space illustrates how the role of the evaluator changes under such conditions. Almost all evaluation

NEW DIRECTIONS FOR EVALUATION • DOI: 10.1002/ev

texts provide clear and useful guidance for evaluators, from novice to expert; if they follow this guidance, evaluators can expect to complete at least a competent study. In contested spaces, evaluators must know about and know how to do an evaluation study as if the context was not contested, and also, they have to know when to modify these general guidelines to make judgments based on the realities on the ground. Here it is not enough that the evaluators have only technical knowledge (how to design and do an evaluation); they also must know what to do and how to complete an evaluation under these tense and dangerous conditions.

Conflict: The Irish at War

In 2003, the Ulster Museum, the national museum in Belfast, Northern Ireland, launched a new exhibition, *Conflict: The Irish at War*. The exhibition focused on the history of conflict in Ireland, going back 10,000 years. It included numerous artifacts and accounts, many of them on loan from community groups and individual residents, as well as several interactive displays within the exhibition that actively encouraged visitor participation (e.g., a wall of visitors' comments that changed regularly as more and more comments were provided) (Bignad, 2011). It also included a collection of firsthand accounts from Northern Ireland residents about what it was like to live and grow up in Northern Ireland. Most visitors, curators, and local residents talked about the inclusion of artifacts and accounts from the time period known as The Troubles, the period beginning in 1968 and ending around the time of the peace accords—called the Good Friday Agreement—in 1998. The exhibition won critical praise and several awards, including the best exhibition award in 2004, and Irish exhibition of the year award, 2005–2006 (Bignad, 2011).

As with almost every public institution in Northern Ireland, the national museum is not a neutral space. From its beginning it had a reputation as being strongly Protestant/Unionist based (Bignad, 2011). It was seen as an instrument and institution of the British state, and often perceived as space supporting this perspective and for this population. It is not a neutral space, and being hired to design and complete an evaluation of a museum exhibition already created the perception that both the evaluator and the evaluation belong with this group, and not the other, the Catholic/Republican group. This is one clear example of how the evaluation enterprise changes when working in a contested space. Settings and sites, even when it appears to outsiders that they would be neutral spaces, are often occupied spaces.

In March 2004, a request for proposals to evaluate the exhibition was published. I was selected to evaluate the exhibition in late summer, and began evaluating in early fall 2004. The evaluation followed a mixed-method design gathering qualitative and quantitative data on the following:

1. The experience of those who perceive themselves as victims of The Troubles
2. The success of the voices technique in terms of perceived satisfaction, engagement, and learning
3. Visitor perceptions of what they learned from the exhibition
4. Visitor enjoyment and satisfaction with the exhibition and the contemplation area

Over a 9-month period, visitors to the exhibition were asked to participate in focus-group interviews and complete surveys as they were visiting the exhibition. In addition, visitor comments and reflections on the exhibition were solicited in the contemplation area at the end of the exhibition. These data were analyzed and interim and final reports were produced. A public presentation on the evaluation was made at the museum.

Evaluation Advisory Group

In designing and carrying out this evaluation of the conflict exhibition the evaluator met regularly with a small group of professionals from that museum. This group included a history curator, a museum outreach officer, and the supervisor of the exhibition. The group provided advice on the design, data collection, analysis, and final reporting, as well as on how to approach visitors at the exhibit respectfully. In addition to these group meetings, the outreach officer and history curator met individually with the evaluator several times over the year-long evaluation to provide feedback and assistance on the evaluation process in the museum and on the Northern Ireland contexts.

In his first meeting with the evaluation advisory group, the focus was on evaluation design, on how to best approach visitors in the exhibition to complete a simple survey, and how to invite participation in focus groups on the exhibition. Overall, the advisory group appreciated the active survey design, where the evaluator would ask visitors in the exhibition to fill out a survey in person, rather than simply leaving surveys in the exhibition for visitors to pick up and fill out. They believed that very few visitors would complete a short survey unless they were invited personally to do so. They talked about the low response rate often associated with passive evaluation design, especially on controversial topics in Northern Ireland. They also provided advice on how to recruit focus-group participants. It was agreed that both the evaluator and the outreach officer would work to arrange focus-group interviews. This proved to be essential, because in the end, the evaluator failed when working alone.

In later meetings with the advisory group, conversations were about both the sharing of preliminary data and ways to continue gathering data to complete the study. At the beginning of the study, the advisory group learned that most respondents were international visitors. The group recommended a focus on gathering more information from local residents and suggested how to do this more efficiently, for example, particular times during the day and week when Northern Ireland residents more often visited the museum. As preliminary data were analyzed and findings emerged, the advisory group provided advice on how to present the data to facilitate its use by museum staff and external funders. This included reorganizing data, and presenting findings of interest to museum staff early in the report, and presenting focus-group quotes and survey data as a single section to add depth to survey findings and make reports more engaging to read.

Finally, the evaluation advisory group ensured that the evaluation would be completed by how they responded to and diffused challenges and obstacles that arose, some typical of any study and some specific to Northern Ireland. They were keenly aware of needing to locate and survey a purposeful sample, so as to guarantee the inclusion of a broad spectrum of voices from across this divided and contested society. They also negotiated with museum staff to allow the evaluator easy access to the exhibition and visitors by providing him with a museum staff badge. The badge quickly demonstrated that the evaluator was working in an official capacity and had the museum's approval to interview visitors. This facilitated easy access to the exhibition and allowed the evaluator to work without interruption by museum security, who would otherwise question the evaluator about what he was doing in the exhibition space talking to museum visitors.

The evaluation advisory group was also instrumental in securing access to data sources that were not immediately available to the evaluator. For example, one such source was anonymous visitor comments left in the contemplation area of the exhibition. Comments were written on index cards and dropped into a secure box. These were regularly collected, and museum curators would select some to be publically displayed in the contemplation area. At first, gaining access to the entire set of cards left by visitors proved difficult. The advisory group facilitated access and negotiated use with the museum staff; therefore the evaluator was provided access to all of the comment cards.

This advisory group was unique in its formation. Rather than the evaluator being responsible for recruiting and creating it, the group was provided to him. This was both advantageous and disadvantageous for the evaluation study and for the evaluator. On the positive side, the advisory group was committed to and interested in learning about the evaluation and to using what was learned. It was easy to bring the group together and their enthusiasm provided additional support to the overall project, especially when the work encountered challenges. They advocated for the evaluation, and willingly shared what was being learned with colleagues both within and outside of the museum. Their very enthusiasm also worked to create additional challenges for the evaluator and for the study.

NEW DIRECTIONS FOR EVALUATION • DOI: 10.1002/ev

With their high interest in the evaluation, the group often asked the evaluator to expand data collection to include additional focus groups or surveys, and to do more data analysis to describe different possible connections between visitor characteristics and experiences. For example, and as noted, when the initial surveys were analyzed, it was learned that most visitors were not residents of Northern Ireland, but rather international visitors and tourists. This both surprised and concerned the evaluation advisory group because they wanted to know about the experiences, learning, and satisfaction of local residents. The evaluator was asked to gather additional surveys and to conduct additional focus-group interviews to increase local participation. He willingly took on the additional work in part as a way to recognize the necessary help of the advisory group to the project.

Discussion

Although the advisory group was not formed by the evaluator, he did utilize it to ensure that the evaluation was implemented, completed, and used. The evaluation advisory group gave legitimacy and access to the evaluator and the study, and addressed issues of and provided political protection to both. It also provided safety to the evaluator and participants who grew up and lived in the very contested space the exhibition was about.

The evaluation advisory group helped address issues of neutrality and bias in the study by supporting an active survey design, arranging, and at times, organizing focus-group interviews, and ensuring full disclosure and access to data sources within the museum. The active survey collection increased the number of surveys completed, and allowed and supported the evaluator in actively seeking out local respondents. The group also arranged focus groups with stakeholder groups that might otherwise not have been included, due to the limited time of the evaluator at the museum. Further, it ensured an open data process by advocating for all visitor responses to be made available for analysis. All of these actions served to give credibility to overall evaluation findings and conclusions, and supported the evaluator's recommendations to extend the time of the exhibit. By ensuring that all stakeholders were included in the evaluation, the final report had greater credibility, both within the museum and within the larger community. Without the inclusion of all local perspectives and feedback on the exhibition, funders and museum staff, as well as local community stakeholders, could have easily dismissed the final evaluation report as not representative and inclusive of all local perspectives.

The advisory group also made the evaluation safer for both the evaluator and participants. The group arranged for a museum staff badge and introduced the evaluator to both security and other museum staff. The evaluator was given institutional support, which in this study meant supporting extensive and effective data collection. The advisory-group members, especially the Outreach Officer, also helped to ensure safety in the focus groups. As someone known and trusted within the community, she could assure participants that their opinions mattered and would be kept confidential by the evaluator. With her support, the evaluator was able to arrange and conduct many more focus-group interviews than what would have been possible. Finally, the advisory-group members increased safety by ensuring that diverse perspectives and multiple voices were included in the evaluation. Almost all stakeholder groups were included, thereby ensuring no single group could claim they were excluded; in that contested context, such perceived "exclusion" could lead to political manipulation and even violence.

All of these actions by the advisory group also provided political protection to the evaluator and for the evaluation process. The evaluator was allowed to work with relative freedom in the museum, and to approach and interview any willing visitor (very few declined). The evaluation study and report were seen as credible because it included people from the two major communities (Catholic/Republican and Protestant/Unionist) in Northern Ireland, and because it spoke directly to their experiences of the exhibition, especially issues they had with how particular recent events and artifacts were handled. Everyone had a chance to respond. Finally, because the advisory group demanded that the evaluator have full and complete access to all data, the report included an analysis of all comments, including those that were critical of the exhibition. In doing so, the report included and described the negative reactions visitors had to the exhibition and discussed how few negative reactions there were overall, as well as how both ethnic/religious communities overwhelmingly viewed the exhibition as well done. The exhibition was not seen to favor one community or another and the evaluation was seen to not favor one community or the other. This would not have been as strong without access to this data source. And in that contested space, this proved rare, unusual, and important for the museum.

Conclusion

This case study illustrates the value of having an evaluation advisory group when doing evaluations in contested space. Although the evaluation advisory group was not intentionally formed, the evaluator did intentionally use it to strengthen the overall evaluation study and report. As this case study shows, the evaluation advisory group provided advice and support throughout the process with members providing advice that strengthened the study and its use. Also by their actions, they increased the safety for the evaluator and study participants. This worked to increase the credibility of the entire process (from design to reporting), by addressing important issues of neutrality; this in turn provided necessary political protection and diffused potential political challenges to the study. As a result, the exhibit,

Conflict: The Irish at War, did not engender any obvious conflict, and in this small way, contributed to the still-lasting peace in that still-contested space.

References

Baizerman, M. (2012). Introduction. *Evaluation and Program Planning, 35*(1), 139–147.

Bignad, K. (2011). How is Ulster's history represented in Northern Ireland museums? The cases of the Ulster folk museum and the Ulster museum. *E-REA, 8*(3). doi: 10.4000/erea.1769

Hargie, O., & Dickson, D. (Eds.) (2003). *Researching the troubles: Social science perspectives on the Northern Ireland conflict.* Edinburgh, Scotland: Mainstream Publishing Ltd.

Harland, K. (2007). The legacy of conflict in Northern Ireland: Paramilitarism, violence, and youthwork in contested spaces. In D. Magnuson & M. Baizerman (Eds.), *Work with youth in divided and contested societies* (pp. 177–190). Rotterdam, Netherlands: Sense Publishing.

Patton, M. Q. (1997). *Utilization-focused evaluation: The new century text* (3rd ed.). Thousand Oaks, CA: Sage.

Sluka, J. (1995). Reflections on managing danger in fieldwork: Dangerous anthropology in Belfast. In C. Nordstrom & A. C. G. M. Robben (Eds.), *Fieldwork under fire: Contemporary studies of violence and survival* (pp. 276–294). Berkeley, CA: University of California Press.

Smyth, M., & Robinson, G. (2001). *Researching violently divided societies: Ethical and methodological issues.* London, England: Pluto Press.

Strocka, C. (2008). Participatory research with war-affected adolescents and youth: Lessons learnt from fieldwork with youth gangs in Ayacucho, Peru. In J. Hart (Ed.), *Years of conflict: Adolescent, political violence and displacement* (pp. 255–276). Oxford, England: Berghahn Books.

VeLure Roholt, R., & Baizerman, M. (2012). Being practical, being safe: Doing evaluations in contested spaces. *Evaluation and Program Planning, 35*(1), 206–217.

Weiss, C. (1993). Where politics and evaluation research meet. *Evaluation Practice, 14*(1), 93–106.

Worthen, B., Sanders, J., & Fitzpatrick, J. (1997). *Program evaluation: Alternative approaches and practical guidelines.* New York, NY: Longman.

ROSS VELURE ROHOLT is an assistant professor in the School of Social Work at the University of Minnesota.

Richards-Schuster, K. (2012). Empowering the voice of youth: The role of youth advisory councils in grant making focused on youth. In R. VeLure Roholt & M. L. Baizerman (Eds.), *Evaluation advisory groups. New Directions for Evaluation, 136,* 87–100.

6

Empowering the Voice of Youth: The Role of Youth Advisory Councils in Grant Making Focused on Youth

Katie Richards-Schuster

Abstract

This article will focus on the potential role for youth evaluation advisory groups within youth grant-making organizations and networks. The main elements to be discussed include the formation of the network, the training program elements, some specific examples of efforts by young people to create and strengthen evaluation within their YACs (youth advisory councils), and the lessons learned. ©Wiley Periodicals, Inc., and the American Evaluation Association.

The construction of youth voice and youth participation in advice-giving roles remains an important issue for discussion. Despite increasing efforts to engage young people in this way and increasing scholarship on the topic, youth participation is still marginalized in society. In general, American society, through its policies and practices, tends to focus on the construction of youth as vulnerable and at risk at best, and as problems at worst (Finn, 2001; Finn & Checkoway, 1998). This construction has lead to a resistance to the idea of including young people as policy,

Special thanks is given to Cheryl Elliott, president and CEO of the Ann Arbor Area Community Foundation, for her feedback, comments, and support of this case study.

program, and evaluator advisors, especially for the most marginalized and disconnected youth. As a result, youth programs tend to focus on protecting or fixing young people's problems rather than on the assets and contributions that young people can make to society (Camino & Zeldin, 2002; Checkoway & Richards-Schuster, 2002, 2006; Finn, 2001; Finn & Checkoway, 1998; Zeldin et al., 2001).

In contrast is a perspective that views young people as competent citizens with a right and responsibility to engage in their communities. This perspective makes the assumption that youth participation provides a legitimate source of information and ideas for making policy, planning, and program decisions, for young people have everyday experiences that position them to "provide a different lens" (Noguera, 2003, p. 135) and "raise issues . . . that might not have otherwise been on the radar of adults" (Endo, 2002, p. 3). This perspective assumes that democracy is strengthened through the participation and active engagement of all people—including young people—in the process (Camino & Zeldin, 2002; Checkoway, 1998; Checkoway et al., 2003; Checkoway, Allison, & Montoya, 2005; Checkoway & Gutierrez, 2006; Checkoway & Richards-Schuster, 2002, 2006).

This perspective, albeit growing in practice and scholarship, still challenges dominant-society paradigms and creates the potential for the shifting of power dynamics within organizations and communities. As such, efforts to engage young people in these ways are still generally seen as exceptions rather than the norm in communities, and many adults are still resistant to the idea and practice of including young people as policy, program, and evaluator advisors.

Youth participation in philanthropy represents a model for exploring questions about youth voice in advice-giving roles. Over the last 20 years, there have been a number of efforts by large foundations, community foundations, and organizations to engage young people in having a voice in the process of grant decisions (Falk & Nissan, 2007; Tice, 2004, Youth Leadership Institute, 2001).

Youth participation of this type includes efforts by youth grant makers affiliated with community foundations to assess community needs for grant-making priorities, establish procedures for grantees to evaluate their activities and outcomes, and evaluate the effectiveness of themselves and their grant-making.

Efforts to engage young people in philanthropy have at their core the concept that youth participation is good for grant making and that their voice contributes to perspective on youth needs, provides information for program planning and decision making, and improves the overall community. In addition, youth participation of this type strengthens social development of young people and prepares them for active participation in a democratic society (Falk & Nissan, 2007; Checkoway et al., 2003; Tice, 2004).

Because of their uniqueness as a model for youth participation that is growing and thriving, these types of youth participation provide a case for examining best practices around how youth advisory boards function, how they can be sustained, and how they can empower youth voice within communities.

This chapter explores these questions through the lens of a statewide youth grant-making network, with focus given to a specific example of a youth advisory council within a community foundation. The data from this case study draw from organization documentation and the author's experience as a staff advisor to the Ann Arbor Area Community Foundation Youth Council from 2002–2005.

Background and History

In the late 1980s, the W. K. Kellogg Foundation launched a challenge grant program as a commitment to growing community foundations and strengthening youth participation. The challenge grant sought to grow existing or create new community foundation endowments through a 2:1 match; for every 2 million dollars a community foundation could raise for its endowment, the W. K. Kellogg Foundation would provide 1 million dollars to each foundation to fund a youth endowment that would be advised by a youth committee. In this step, the W. K. Kellogg Foundation provided a permanent vehicle for youth participation within community foundations across the state of Michigan. Known as Youth Advisory Committees (YACs), these committees created roles for young people to have an active voice in grant making in their communities. Although YACs were structured in various forms based on the individual community foundations, all YACs were expected to (a) conduct needs assessments every 3 years to identify needs and determine grant priorities, (b) promote volunteerism and philanthropy in youth, and (c) make grant recommendations rooted in youth needs and determined priorities (Mawby, 1991).

Growth of a Statewide Network

Since the first YACs in Michigan began in the late 1980s, over 80 YACs have been formed to represent youth participation in almost every community foundation in the state. Although each YAC is structured slightly differently, the majority engages 15–20 diverse young people of high school age from the local community. Emphasis is placed on recruiting a group of young people that reflects the diversity of the community rather than a sole focus on traditional youth leaders. The goal of diversity is to ensure that the group includes a broad set of perspectives from the community. The community-based YACs meet regularly to engage in grant making, service, and leadership activities.

The Michigan Community Foundation Youth Grant Making Project (MCFYP) was developed within the Council of Michigan Foundations to support the emergence of YACs within community foundations. MCFYP developed a committee of youth grant makers, supported by a Council of Michigan Foundations CMF staff person, who was charged with building capacity of youth grant makers in related activities and the capacity of adult advisors to work with young people. In addition, MCFYP provided an annual leadership conference and annual regional workshops to promote special topics and build capacity of youth grant makers on special issues including grant making, leadership, stewardship, and evaluation. This was done to build young people's capacity in advice giving and grant making.

Early in its development, CMF and MCFYP recognized the importance of adult advisors to the success of the YACs. Adults were essential to being able to support the youth grant makers, provide leadership training, and serve as a bridge linking the youth leaders with other adults in the community. Special training was developed to support adults in addition to creating a network for adult advisors to share ideas and lessons learned.

Youth Grant Making in Action

The Ann Arbor Area Community Foundation YAC, called the Youth Council, began in 1989 through the W. K. Kellogg Challenge Grant. Over the last 23 years, the Youth Council has created a space for young people to engage in grant-making efforts, strengthen the role of young people as leaders, and promote philanthropy and volunteerism in the community.

The Youth Council involves 20–25 young people of high school age, which aims to reflect the diversity of the Ann Arbor community. Members are recruited from across the community and generally represent the breadth of the various public and private high schools in the community to ensure all voices are represented on the councils. The process of selection is youth led. Interested youth complete an application and participate in a peer-interview process. Once selected, youth members are asked to stay on until they complete high school. In the last 22 years, there have only been a handful of young people that have left the Youth Council for reasons other than moving. In part this commitment reflects the strong engagement of the youth and the fact that they find the Youth Council a meaningful activity for them. When asked, many of the young people talk about the importance of their voice in grant-making decisions and their role as leaders in the community.

The Youth Council meets monthly. It is advised by a part-time staff member who provides overall guidance, feedback, and training, and serves as a liaison between the youth, the community foundation staff, and the Board of Trustees. A youth leadership team that includes cochairs, a secretary, a Board of Trustee member, and a Board of Trustee-in-Training leads the Youth Council. Youth Council members select their own leadership team through a nomination and vote process. The leadership team meets with the advisor regularly throughout the month to discuss process, set meeting agendas, develop leadership and training needs, and organize Youth Council activities.

New Directions for Evaluation • DOI: 10.1002/ev

The inclusion of a Youth Council Trustee, a full voting member of the Board, was a testament to the importance of youth voice by the Foundation. The development of a Youth Trustee position was linked to the 1999 passage of a state "Youth on Boards Bill" that lowered the age in which people could serve as voting members of boards of directors from 18 to 16 years of age. The Council of Michigan strongly advocated for the legislation crafted in collaboration with youth members of the MCFYP committee. The Ann Arbor Area Community Foundation's first Youth Council Trustee member began her term in 1999. In every year since then, a young person has been selected to serve on the Board and participate in all decisions and voting rights as any adult member.

After the first few years, the Community Foundation developed a Trustee-in-Training role to provide a year of training before the youth assumes her/his voting role. This was done as a result of an exit interview with the then Youth Trustee, who raised the idea of a "training year" for youth members that would help the new Trustee to understand the complexities of the Ann Arbor Area Community Foundation and, as an extra benefit, be another young person at largely adult meetings. The Trustee-in-Training is typically selected in her/his junior year and is expected to attend all Board functions and meetings but does not have a vote in Community Foundation operations. In the following year, the youth is elected to the Board of Trustees and assumes all rights and roles as any other adult Board Trustee. Over the years, the Community Foundation learned that having at least two young people serving on an adult board helps provide mutual support and helps encourage participation. The ability to have a year of training also supports the Youth Trustee to be prepared to engage in the real decision-making needs of the Board. Youth are assumed to be active, not token, members of the Board of Trustees.

The major responsibility of the Youth Council is to make recommendations on grants that have been requested from the Community Foundation's Youth Fund. This occurs twice per year. The grant requests that come to the Youth Fund are first reviewed by Community Foundation staff for fit and for appropriate documentation; then the majority of the review and selection process is done by the Youth Council. During the actual grant process, Youth Council members review proposals, conduct interviews, and make recommendations on proposals and budgets. Per the terms of the W. K. Kellogg grant, all recommendations go through the Board of Trustees, as is the case with all grant proposals.

In preparation for the grant process, the Youth Council conducts leadership and grant-making training for its members. Among the training activities include discussing issues and setting priorities, assessing grant proposals, and reading budgets. The members also conduct sample grant-making review processes to practice and discuss critical issues.

Over the last 23 years, the Youth Council also has engaged in various activities to raise the voice of young people within the Community Foundation and the community. For example, the Youth Council has led community forums on youth topics and special grant initiatives based on youth priorities. And they created a forum on youth–adult partnerships in the community and coauthored a proposal to create a comprehensive youth advisory council for a neighboring community. They led a mapping of activities and related focus groups to understand what teens wanted in after-school hours. Their findings, in conjunction with a community-wide feasibility study, led to the development of a challenge grant to launch a teen center that, 13 years later, continues to thrive as an organizational hub for youth engagement efforts in the community. Over the years, the Youth Council's efforts have encouraged, funded, and provided technical assistance to other organizations interested in engaging young people in advisory roles. As a result of their efforts, young people are advisors to local nonprofits; create youth-led leadership committees within organizations; and serve on committees for various school, city, and country government bodies. In addition, the Youth Council regularly supports youth philanthropy activities by engaging in community service and community-wide efforts aimed at promoting volunteerism among youth.

Infusing Evaluation Into Youth Grant-Making Efforts

Evaluation has been an important component to the Youth Council and to the Community Foundation since its inception. Although there had always been a variety of evaluation mechanisms in place, during the early to mid-2000s there was a strengthened focus of evaluation by the Youth Council. In part this focus came from discussion about the importance of fidelity and also from a push by the larger MCFYP statewide network to encourage evaluation within youth grant making.

When discussed by the Youth Council, the members talked about evaluation as important for the following reasons: (a) it was the responsibility of the Youth Council to evaluate itself, its programs, and community; (b) it was the right of young people to be part of asking questions and gathering information about their community; (c) it was important for creating a history and documentation for other young people; (d) it was essential to ascertain the impact that the Youth Council and its grant making was having on the community; and (e) it was important to use the information to inform efforts and create changes in the community.

Although the Youth Council already conducted evaluation through grantee reports, community assessments, and general evaluation at the end of each year, the group decided to create a more systematic approach to its evaluation. As noted above, the Youth Council felt evaluation was critical to helping them increase the credibility of their advice and recommendation. Evaluation was a vehicle for them to show how seriously they took this work and the importance of being careful and systematic in their responsiveness to community needs.

NEW DIRECTIONS FOR EVALUATION • DOI: 10.1002/ev

To do so, the Council formed a standing committee of three to four members. The members of the committee were selected by the leadership team for their interest in evaluation and represented a small subset of the overall Council. In addition, the leadership team appointed one member of the committee to help move evaluation efforts forward. The evaluation committee met regularly, inside and outside of meetings, to develop plans. The committee focused on evaluation in three ways: conducting internal evaluation of the Youth Council, conducting external evaluation of the grantees and the community, and using the information gathered for improving processes and prioritizing issues for action.

The internal evaluation efforts focused on documenting and assessing the work of the Youth Council. The goal for the internal efforts was to create a record of the activities, make program adjustments, and think more critically about their own process. Examples of activities that were developed included conducting periodic surveys of Youth Council members on meeting quality, program activities desired, and training and recruitment activities; holding debriefings (what went well, not so well, and improvements for next time) after events to ensure that evaluative information was documented for future planning; and creating an annual scrapbook to document the year's work through photographs, minutes, program activity materials, and write-ups about events and lessons learned. The internal evaluation efforts were used to improve grant-making practices, to improve meeting quality, and to capture the efforts of the Youth Council for the next year. For example, after an evaluation of the Youth Council meetings suggested that there was not enough opportunity for discussion, the leadership team developed strategies to make meetings more participatory and created committees to support small-group discussions within meetings.

The external evaluation efforts focused on understanding the community and assessing the impact of the Youth Council on the community. Examples of external evaluation included revamping grantee evaluation reports, conducting interviews with grantees, and engaging in grant-making site visits to assess impact.

Another component of the external evaluation was assessing community needs and issues. This aspect of evaluation was a component of the initial W. K. Kellogg Foundation funds that required youth grant makers to evaluate their communities' issues and priorities every 3 years. Through the grant-making committee, the Youth Council strengthened their approach by gathering comprehensive survey and interview data to assess community issues. For example, in 1 year, the Youth Council developed a comprehensive needs assessment, which involved a traditional survey approach and a video documentary to explore issues raised in the survey, and provided a vehicle for communicating their findings. The group analyzed their survey findings and then brainstormed additional questions and areas for information gathering. The youth brainstormed about people (youth and adults) to be interviewed and then reached out to ask the people to participate.

NEW DIRECTIONS FOR EVALUATION • DOI: 10.1002/ev

In total, 30 youth and adults were interviewed. The video clips were then analyzed for topics and themes. The Youth Council was able to include survey findings in the video to support and illuminate the interviewee quotes. The final video was shown in the community to generate discussion and used to inform its members and the broader foundation staff and Board of Trustees about youth issues in the community. Over the years, the Youth Council has used their assessment findings to develop community-wide forums on priority topics such as youth–parent communication, teen stress, and youth leadership. These forums served as another vehicle for the Youth Council to have a voice in advising and lifting up key issues and providing a platform for youth and adults to come together around youth needs in the community.

To prepare for evaluation activities, the youth committee attended workshops and trainings sponsored by the MCFYP on evaluation. This included network-wide training and statewide conference experiences and small intensive trainings focused on developing and strengthening evaluation plans. For example, after attending a MCFYP training, the youth developed an hour-long training on evaluation, which they conducted at the orientation retreat. The training included a focus on understanding the what and why of evaluation, steps in the process, asking questions, and practicing conducting site visits. During the training, the YAC members developed questions to be used as part of a site-visit protocol. Following the training, YAC members conducted site visits with the use of the protocol developed. The information gathered was reported back to the whole YAC at an upcoming meeting, and was used to inform the next grant cycle process.

The youth also drew on the resources of their advisors, who had evaluation experience, and on related information and best practices that they compiled from other youth councils. Some of the evaluation committee members also created simplified forms and training protocols and developed peer-led mini-workshops on interviews, site visits, and survey development. The Youth Council also drew on the experience of past alumni, now in college, for support with surveys and data analysis.

Empowering the Voice of Youth in Grant Making and Advising Community Issues

The Youth Council as an advisory group and the subset evaluation advisory committee have played critical roles in ensuring that youth voices have an opportunity to impact practices, create organizational changes, and raise important community issues.

In many ways, the evaluation committee provided a space to lift up the evaluation efforts and allow for the broader Youth Council to be in a better position to enable youth voices to be heard—both within and beyond the group—because it created systematic approaches for the Youth Council to

NEW DIRECTIONS FOR EVALUATION • DOI: 10.1002/ev

gather information, analyze their findings, and present their ideas. Youth members and adults in the Foundation and the broader community were receptive to ideas and changes developed by the youth, in part because they had been realized through evaluation efforts. Youth members could back up their ideas with facts, numbers, and quotes as evidence of their advice and recommendations. Thus, within the group, the evaluation committee helped build on strengths and identify areas for changes leading to better youth meetings, increased grant-making training, and assessing Youth Council activities and future directions. In addition, the ability to document and assess its activities allowed the group to share their approaches and practices with other youth grant makers. As a result the Youth Council has presented its efforts in statewide and national forums.

The overall Youth Council, as an advisory group, has also been critical for helping the broader Community Foundation set direction, examine needs of young people, and learn lessons from the youth. The Youth Council has helped to ensure that youth are seen as leaders in the community through funding the development of teen advisory boards in area organizations and providing funding to organizations that involve young people in program development and evaluation. It helped create needed partnerships to strengthen youth participation in the region, including the development of an area-wide coalition to increase opportunities for youth philanthropy and civic innovation in a neighboring community. Last, the focus on evaluation, and its use, has allowed for opportunities to use and share their findings with the community and therefore highlight critical issues facing youth. Overall, the youth council has helped to pave the way in the community for the role of young people and the ways young people can advise and set direction on practices and possibilities.

Implications and Best Practices

Young people should participate in advisory boards and committees, and this is especially true within foundations. Young people can and should have a voice in evaluating critical issues facing youth, advising the direction of grant making to address those issues, and strengthening programming and activities for young people in the community. As this case study makes clear, they can provide good advice—advice that is taken seriously because it includes multiple perspectives and is based in evidence. Evaluation further supported the credibility of their recommendations and other advice giving because it was a critical role in this process. Young people should have an opportunity for assessing their own programs and structures, asking questions about the community, and developing information that can be used for action. Overall, youth participation promotes the accountability of youth philanthropy and the foundations of which they are part.

Youth participation of this type, however, requires special understanding about process and best practices, as it can vary in implementation.

NEW DIRECTIONS FOR EVALUATION • DOI: 10.1002/ev

Often the literature assesses participation through the lens of "authentic participation" or "meaningful participation" (Hart, 1992). In these cases, participation is not measured by the quantity of young people or numbers of activities, but rather by the quality of the participation, the level of engagement, and the ability for young people to have an authentic role in the process (Checkoway et al., 2003).

As youth grant advisory boards and youth evaluation advisory groups emerge, it will be critical for efforts to understand a basic set of principles about youth participation. To that end, there are a number of best practice documents that detail critical components needed to support youth as grant makers and youth evaluation.

Over the last 20 years, the MCFYP Council developed a set of best practices around youth philanthropy (see www.youthgrantmakers.org for more information). Many of the best practices, culled from lessons learned from various YACs, provide guides for the general development, support, and sustainability of such councils. The website lists 14 best practices for Youth Advisory Councils, including the following:

1. Meets a minimum of seven times a year.
2. Has a minimum of 12 members ages 12–21 who reflect the many forms of diversity found in the local youth community.
3. Has two trained YAC advisors provided by the community foundation who are knowledgeable and supportive of youth development and youth leadership.
4. Holds an annual orientation for all new members and encourages all members to participate in training opportunities that will strengthen their skills in philanthropy.
5. Assesses critical issues of area youth at least every 3 years.
6. Engages in a grant-making process that is responsive to the critical issues of area youth annually.
7. Evaluates the effectiveness of each grant annually.
8. Participates in a community youth project annually.
9. Engages in fund development activities to assist with the continual growth of the endowed youth fund and the community foundation annually.
10. Has at least one YAC member serving as a full voting member on the community foundation Board of Trustees.
11. Interacts with community foundation board, staff, and donors regularly on a formal and informal level.
12. Has activities highlighted in the community foundation's annual report, website, newsletters, public presentations, and other communication tools.
13. Conducts an annual self-assessment to reflect upon its strengths, challenges, use of best practices, and opportunities for improvement.
14. Participates in and attends the Youth Grant Makers Summer Leadership Conference, Fall Regional Trainings, and Advisor Roundtables.

NEW DIRECTIONS FOR EVALUATION • DOI: 10.1002/ev

In addition, sparked by a 2007 Wingspread Conference on Youth Participation in Public Policy, a group of scholars and practitioners worked to develop a set of underlying principles and values for youth participation (Sedonean, O'Doherty, Richards-Schuster, Ordeloa, & Jackson, n.d.). At the core of these concepts is valuing young people as advisors and leaders in the community, providing authentic opportunities for young people to engage and advise outcomes, the importance of ongoing opportunities for young people, the need for training and education to support this participation, and the requirement that adults and organizational leaders buy in to the participation of young people in this way, and also provide the support needed for young people to be successful.

These principles highlight the importance of ensuring that young people's advice has meaning and influence and is not tokenized or treated in a decorated way (Arnstein, 1969; Hart, 1992). This is not about solely "adding more chairs to table" (Nyden et al., 1997), but rather the ability to add chairs that also guarantee that the advice of young people will have influence and will affect the conversations, priorities, and decisions made (Checkoway, 1998; Checkoway & Richards-Schuster, 2006).

Youth Advisory Councils provide an especially interesting approach to authentic youth participation and youth advice-making approaches because they are linked to endowed funds. Tying youth participation and advice giving to sustained funding structures through endowed funds ensures that young people have a role in ongoing ways. In addition, through evaluation processes that are tied to the endowed funds, including needs assessments and other internal and external evaluation activities, young people provide a credible body for giving advice and helping shape the priorities of grant making related to youth in the community. Adult buy-in has been essential to the process and was required for the initial funding of the endowments. Over time, as adults connected to foundations have seen the importance of young people's advice in the grant-making process, it has helped reinforce the value of young people in this role. The commitments to evaluation and the training and responsibility taken by the young people, in their role, further enhance their credibility and build trust for their ideas.

Although this case has focused largely on the role of young people in advisory committees within foundations, it highlights some of the basic guidelines for engaging young people in advisory and evaluation advisory groups and provides lessons in future efforts aimed at working with youth on adult-majority evaluation advisory committees and with youth on youth-majority evaluation advisory committees:

1. Young people provide critical perspectives on community. They can and should have a voice and their insight contributes to the overall development of community programs and planning. Critical to the acceptance of young people's participation is having key staff—Executive

Directors, Board Chairs, and key adults—also articulating the importance of youth voice and involvement. Organizational buy-in is crucial to creating sustained opportunities for authentic, nontokenized participation of young people.

2. Adults are essential to the engagement of young people. Too often efforts to engage youth in advisory roles focus solely on the youth without attention to the role of adults in supporting young people. Youth need adults who can be allies to their efforts and can serve as bridge between youth and adults. Advisory boards that engage youth need to take stock of the adults and provide training and education capacity building to support adults who are in this role.

3. Young people, like adults, need adequate training and education for their role. Efforts to engage young people on boards or councils should pay attention to providing the appropriate background information and preparation required to be able to engage in discussions and decision making. This may include attending special workshops, hosting retreats, or providing ongoing opportunities for education.

4. Diversity is important to ensure a broad-based perspective and range of ideas. In majority adult groups, young people bring different insight to the table and help to provide a broader understanding of the needs and issues in the community. Similarly, in youth-led councils, diversity across social identities and interests is essential for the overall discussion and representation of ideas and perspectives. Special attention needs to be paid to facilitating discussion across differences and ensuring that different perspectives are encouraged rather than isolated. In the case of youth on adult majority boards, having at least two young people serve can reduce isolation and build support to encourage participation.

5. Efforts to engage young people should involve a commitment to systematic information gathering in both internal and external evaluation efforts. Youth involvement is important in at least two aspects. First, when young people engage in evaluation efforts, they provide a new perspective through which to view data about the organization and community. As a result, the questions they ask and the information they gather often lead to important insights that strengthen their own efforts and improve programs and policies that impact young people. When this happens, the process of evaluation also empowers young people to have a voice in their community. Second, youth participation in evaluation also lends credibility to their advice and recommendations. When young people can legitimate their ideas in evidence and use data to back up their claims, it helps build trust for the importance of their perspective in decision making, especially in majority-dominated adult boards (Checkoway & Richards-Schuster, 2006).

Conclusion

Young people should participate in advisory committees focused on grant making and evaluation. The efforts in Michigan show this as a promising strategy for youth and community engagement. The impact of their participation shapes grant-making process, organizational structures, and the voice of young people in community issues. Evaluation advisory subcommittees further enhance the voice of young people by enabling them to assess their own functioning, learn from their experiences, and survey the issues in the broader community. The potential of these types of advisory structures, however, is limited by how participation is conceptualized and structured. As evidenced by the case example, participation needs to be valued, engaged, structured, and supported. And, when young people can be supported and adults can serve as allies, youth voices can be empowered in ways that can lead to organizational and community changes.

References

Arnstein, S. (1969). A ladder of citizen participation. *Journal of the American Institute of Planners, 35,* 216–224.

Camino, L., & Zeldin, S. (2002). From periphery to center: Pathways for youth civic engagement in the day-to-day life of communities. *Applied Developmental Science,* 6(4), 213–220.

Checkoway, B. (1998). Involving young people in neighborhood development. *Children and Youth Services Review, 20*(9/10), 765–795.

Checkoway, B., Allison, A., & Montoya, C. (2005). Youth participation in public policy at the municipal level. *Children and Youth Services Review, 27,* 1149–1162.

Checkoway, B., & Gutierrez, L. (2006). Youth participation and community change: An introduction. *Journal of Community Practice, 14*(1/2).

Checkoway, B., & Richards-Schuster, K. (2002). Lifting new voices for socially just communities. *Community Youth Development,* 2(4), 32–37.

Checkoway, B., & Richards-Schuster, K. (2006). Youth participation for educational reform in low-income communities of color. In P. Noguera, S. Ginwright, & J. Cammarota (Eds.), *Beyond resistance: Youth activism and community change: New democratic possibilities for policy and practice for America's youth.* New York, NY: Routledge.

Checkoway, B., Richards-Schuster, K., Abdullah, S., Aragon, M., Facio, E., Figueroa, L., … Welsh, M. (2003). Young people as competent citizens. *Community Development Journal: An International Forum, 38*(4), 298–309.

Endo, T. (2002). *Youth engagement in community-driven school reform.* Oakland, CA: Social Policy Research Associates.

Falk, K., & Nissan, L. (2007). A vision for and brief history of youth philanthropy. *American Fundraising Professionals, 1.*

Finn, J. (2001). Text and turbulence: Representing adolescence as pathology in the human services. *Childhood, 8*(2), 167–191.

Finn, J., & Checkoway, B. (1998). Young people as competent community builders: A challenge to social work. *Social Work, 43*(4), 335–345.

Hart, R. (1992). *Children's participation from tokenism to citizenship.* Florence, Italy: UNICEF International Child Development Centre.

Mawby, R. (1991). Why youth? Why community foundations? Keynote address delivered by Dr. Russell G. Mawby, Chairman of the W. K. Kellogg Foundation, June 21,

1991. Michigan Youth Community Foundation Project Best Practices. Retrieved from www.youthgrantmakers.org

Noguera, P. (2003). *City schools and the American dream: Reclaiming the promise of public education.* New York, NY: Teachers College Press.

Nyden, P., Figert, A., Shibley, M., & Burrows, D. (1997). *Building community: Social science in action.* Thousand Oaks, CA: Pine Forge Press.

Sedonean, M., O'Doherty, R., Richards-Schuster, K., Ordeloa, A., & Jackson, J. (n.d.). *Youth participation in public policy.* Unpublished working paper.

Tice, K. (2004). *Leadership, volunteerism and giving: A longitudinal study of youth grantmakers (1993–2003).* Grand Haven, MI: Council of Michigan Foundations.

Youth Leadership Institute. (2001). *Changing the face of giving: An assessment of youth philanthropy.* San Francisco, CA: The James Irvine Foundation.

Zeldin, S., McDaniel, A., Topitzes, D., & Calvert, M. (2001). *Youth in decision-making: A study on the impacts of youth on adults and organizations.* Washington, DC: Innovation Center for Community Youth Development.

KATIE RICHARDS-SCHUSTER *is an assistant research scientist, Michigan Youth and Community Program, School of Social Work, University of Michigan.*

Block, B. B. (2012). Congratulations on the new initiative! Is it time for a new committee? In R. VeLure Roholt & M. L. Baizerman (Eds.), *Evaluation advisory groups. New Directions for Evaluation, 136,* 101–108.

7

Congratulations on the New Initiative! Is It Time for a New Committee?

Betsy Baum Block

Abstract

United Way of the Bay Area (UWBA) has started to implement its 10-year initiative: Cut Poverty in Half in the Bay Area by 2020, in partnership with hundreds of organizations. The goal is audacious, and the effort required immense. As a founding steering council begins to move forward with all the complexities of this initiative, among the many challenges is to answer how our progress and impact can feasibly be measured. The concept of an evaluation advisory committee (EAC) holds tremendous appeal as a way to leverage the best experts to provide critical input and help us define credible evidence for success. In developing the EAC, we found no ready-made guide and began constructing our own approach. This chapter discusses considerations for the framework of an EAC, and shares some key decisions about its purpose and structure. It shares our initial goals, the proposed composition of the EAC, and how our understanding of engaging an EAC has evolved. © Wiley Periodicals, Inc., and the American Evaluation Association.

U nited Way of the Bay Area (UWBA), along with hundreds of community partners, will work to cut in half the number of Bay Area families living in poverty by 2020. UWBA convened an initial group as a founding steering council, leveraging the collective-impact framework and organizations that have track records of addressing poverty and driving effective community-change initiatives. The collective-impact model is defined as a set of partners adopting a common agenda, along with shared measurement of their work, undertaking mutually reinforcing activities, maintaining constant communication, and investing in an administrative backbone to drive the ongoing work of the partnership (Kania & Kramer, 2011).

Partners in UWBA's work to cut poverty in half by 2020 cross multiple sectors—nonprofit, public, philanthropic, and private—and have expressed a deep commitment to achieve this goal. Through the initial stage, UWBA has committed its staff for the backbone role and provided an initial road map, coordinating communication among partners and providing the logistical support to convene all the partners at regular meetings.

Before bringing partners to the table, UWBA spent considerable time selecting a definition of poverty. The definition was built from UWBA's work with the self-sufficiency standard, the input heard during the 30 focus groups conducted during a community conversations process in 2010, and a short set of meetings with a handful of partners to begin framing the metrics conversation. Refining this definition will not only better define our target population and give us a truer baseline, but also measure the impact we anticipate our efforts will have. The draft road map, as it gets refined and adopted by our partners, offers a starting point for evaluation, but will require much more input and guidance to become a comprehensive plan.

This chapter will focus on our creation of an evaluation advisory council (EAC) to capture outcomes and data that will inform our efforts during the initiative's formative stages. Accordingly, this article is intended to pose questions rather than provide strong guidance. We have focused our questions regarding the structure of the EAC and its products. The goals of the EAC and how they are accomplished is a story waiting to be told.

Evaluation Challenges in Past Community-Change Initiatives

The Cut Poverty initiative builds on the strengths of the community-change initiative field, and the effective use of data and evaluation is a central tenet of this work. Evaluation can guide the leaders in defining a problem, as well as ensuring that work can be measured and progress tracked. Evaluation also makes sure the work stays accountable to its stakeholders. In addition, it can be an important tool for engaging community residents (David, 2008; Meehan, Casteneda & Salvesen, 2011). The literature on community-change evaluation has grown over the last 10 years, and shifts evaluation to the other end of the spectrum—from the typical outcomes-driven evaluation of programs to increased focus on directly measuring the social and economic progress an initiative can achieve (Kubisch et al., 2002). Evaluators have written about the multitude of challenges presented by this new type of evaluation:

- The fluidity of an initiative's evolution
- A complex group of stakeholders
- Multiple purposes for the findings
- The initiative's propensity to grow, both horizontally (across institutions) and vertically (across individual, family, and community levels)
- The contextual factors of the community when looking at such a broad set of efforts and outcomes
- The methodological challenges (lack of a control group, selection bias, and spillover to name a few) (Hollister & Hill, 1995; Kubisch et al., 2002)

The challenges listed above are compounded by the natural tensions and unresolved community issues of working with such a broad set of stakeholders, as well as the political and funding dimensions, which are inherent in this type of initiative (Kubisch et al., 2002). To succeed, evaluators need to navigate these challenges and create a set of outcomes that are timely and relevant enough to engage the leadership of an initiative as a learning organization, without sacrificing meaningful outcomes produced with rigor.

A New Movement, and a Missing Piece

UWBA's collaborative effort, Cut Poverty in Half by 2020, will engage hundreds of foundations, nonprofits, and for-profit partners in a seven-county region and will be structured to include the following:

- An overarching steering committee will guide the efforts of all the partners. This Founding Steering Council will kick off the effort, then seat the ongoing Road-Map Steering Council. As shown in Figure 7.1, UWBA anticipates the key levers of the initiative to be fourfold, and driving agreement on a common set of outcomes is a critical lever in this process.
- A backbone organization will provide an administrative infrastructure to manage the ongoing effort, implement the evaluation plan, and manage whatever activities the founding partners define as necessary. UWBA will staff this until the steering group determines the best infrastructure.
- A series of design teams and action teams that target a specific geographic, programmatic, and/or policy area. The groups will both design and implement strategies, supported by the backbone and guided by the Road-Map Steering Council.

UWBA wants to put resources and emphasis on defining and implementing an evaluation plan that makes sense for this effort, and addresses all the levers above—along with the programmatic effects both short and long term. The Founding Steering Council focuses on leaders in the community

Figure 7.1. The Four Key Levers of the Cut Poverty in Half Initiative,
Defined by the Road-Map Steering Council, Supported by a Backbone,
and Implemented by Action Teams

who can influence and rally partners to the table, limiting the input at this
stage of those evaluation experts who can define an evaluation strategy that
addresses many of the challenges complex community-change initiative
evaluations face.

Overall, the effort aims to be results focused and data driven. The
structure includes many moving parts, several varied perspectives, and a
potentially fragmented starting point for answering one seemingly simple
question: Are fewer families in poverty? The question is connected to a
more nuanced evaluation approach, which would consider whether and
how partners' efforts resulted in a reduction in poverty for the individuals
and families who are touched by their interventions.

Keeping Evaluation at the Forefront

In order to keep evaluation at the forefront of the collective efforts of Cut
Poverty in Half by 2020, UWBA asked whether it made sense to create an
EAC as a complementary structure to the initial steering group. The concept of a formal evaluation committee is new to UWBA and merited consideration for how the entire initiative could benefit. Four major
considerations emerged.

Input from a critical stakeholder group could better enable the initiative to adopt a methodology for measuring poverty that goes beyond simply
calculating changes in the poverty rate. The initiative has the best chance
of being successful if we bring many voices to the conversation that can

significantly move ahead the critical thinking of the initiative. Additionally, by working closely with those we anticipate could bring a critical voice in reviewing the findings, we could create the most credible calculation for measuring poverty and its related indicators. Not only does having a credible, well-vetted evaluation methodology benefit the ongoing management of the initiative, it also provides some best practices if another community attempts to replicate a similar initiative.

Inclusion of respected experts could mitigate the need for geographic representation presented by the tremendous variation in the target population. The initiative crosses seven counties that have considerable demographic, economic, and rural/suburban/urban diversity. In addition, our proposed road map includes strategies across the entire life span—early childhood, transition-age youth, adults, and senior citizens. When layering the geographic, population, and programmatic variations, we became concerned about the number of people we would have to invite to make the EAC fully representative of all the stakeholder interests. We envisioned that some groups could feel marginalized or competitive in our conversations about an evaluation approach.

Providing the Founding Steering Council with input from respected experts could facilitate the council taking ownership of the metrics sooner. A key success for the initiative is achieving leadership and ownership by the partners, along with their commitment to define, align their work to, and inform the metrics central to its success. However, the partners have expressed a strong desire to take the fastest road to action, and leverage the backbone work to accelerate planning. The partners realize their commitment to providing data is critical for the ongoing work not just because it helps the initiative, but also because it, in turn, becomes critical to each partner's work. They have asked UWBA to take leadership in providing options for their consideration.

An EAC can serve to build confidence in the partners that the right information and skills are at the table to achieve the goal. By seeking out individuals who are respected voices in the field and bringing them to the conversation to shape the initiative's strategy, UWBA hopes the partners assume a higher degree of confidence in designing the implementation plan.

From this point, UWBA proposed some key framing questions:

- Who has the history, memory, and expertise to shape an evaluation design for a comprehensive community-change initiative that uses a collective-impact framework where the nature of the study is broad, and yet requires tangible, timely data to manage the effort?
- Who can bring experience in the implementation challenges for the methodologies that can be implemented in this evaluation?
- What process will create legitimacy, leadership, and build a solid foundation for a culture of and the practice of evaluation in the initiative?

NEW DIRECTIONS FOR EVALUATION • DOI: 10.1002/ev

Identifying Clear Next Steps

After identifying the potential benefits and considerations of an EAC, UWBA identified some key steps that will be necessary if we are to move ahead with the committee. Although introduced sequentially, the steps in reality occur almost simultaneously and inform each other.

Step 1. Define the goals. We laid out a set of goals for the committee. What is the methodology for determining poverty among those that UWBA and its partners serve? What interim progress indicators should partners use to assess ongoing progress? What data elements should be collected and shared across all the road-map partners?

Step 2. Define the process to convene and facilitate the committee. We initially identified an evaluation firm, and with them considered a one-time convening of national experts that would work through key questions and began to define tangible outcomes. UWBA also considered identifying the EAC as a subset of a steering council or area stakeholders that will meet on an ongoing basis.

Step 3. Define the criteria for inclusion on the committee. The initial list contains more than 40 names; ideally, the EAC will be comprised of fewer than 18 members to allow for fruitful discussion and progress. A diverse committee will ideally include:

- Several individuals who will also serve on the Road-Map Steering Council, so that we create a sense of continuity and connection from what national experts define to what the local leaders need to implement.
- Academics who specialize in poverty measurement.
- Practitioners with experience in direct service for the interventions in the road map.
- Regional and state experts responsible for economic and demographic reporting.
- Measurement and program evaluation experts in different strategies defined in the road map.

Every member of the EAC should feel connected to the goals of the initiative such that their participation is more than a professional obligation. After the initial Founding Steering Council met in March 2012, UWBA began a set of key informational interviews that will help define an approach to be proposed by the Founding Steering Council, and if or how an EAC could be incorporated into the ongoing work to cut poverty in half in the Bay Area by 2020.

The Challenges That Lie Ahead

As we continue the dialogue, with the objective of convening a committee, we still have numerous questions to resolve. Would an initial ad hoc convening or an ongoing EAC best serve the needs of the Founding Steering Council? The structure of collective impact closely ties consideration of outcomes to a council's work, so it is unclear if an adjunct body or a short-term infusion of expertise that will push ahead the Founding Steering Council's work best serves the initiative.

If an ad hoc committee is formed, is a convening of national experts for an EAC worth funding? If we move ahead with a convening of national experts, the initiative would incur travel and expenses as well as additional facilitation costs. Alternatively, the initiative could benefit from a lower-cost meeting of local and regional experts, and leverage evaluation staff at partner agencies or identify a way of engaging national experts on a less-formal advisory basis.

Will we truly be able to bring together this group and create a product that the steering group and partners will want to adopt? Some of the firms that work on evaluating such initiatives give a strong caution to putting people at the helm of the evaluation design who do not actually have a stake in the ongoing work, even if the goal is to produce a straw design that will inform the decision making on an ongoing basis rather than at a one-time convening.

Where should we focus the energy of the committee? Given the proposed scope of the effort, the EAC would need to consider multiple levels of evaluation. This gives some complementary (or conflicting?) objectives. The Founding Steering Council will face a lot of trade-offs between the idealism of integrated case management and real-time data of activities occurring for all of our partners versus the realities of costs and time frames to implement solutions. We also need to consider the biggest bang for the buck on what stories we need to tell—about the overall change in poverty in our seven counties, about the number of people helped and their short-term outcomes, and about the deeper changes in the service-delivery system. We will likely need to prioritize needs, knowing we are unlikely to get enough funding to do it all.

Is attribution to the road-map partners' efforts important? As we determine our approach, we will face the inevitable challenge of causality and attribution. We are actively discussing with our partners if this is truly a question we must answer and how.

Over the next few months, as we seek funding and get closer to seating an EAC, we will start to work through these questions, engaging many of the experts who contributed to our thought process on EACs. At the end of our process, we hope to contribute to others who are at the beginning stages of other, similar initiatives.

References

David, T. (2008). *Community engagement.* Report prepared for The California Endowment. Retrieved from www.tdavid.net/social_change.html

Hollister, R. G., & Hill, J. (1995). Problems in the evaluation of community-wide initiatives. In J. P. Connell, A. C. Kubisch, L. B. Schorr, & C. H. Weiss (Eds.), *New approaches to evaluating community initiatives. Volume 1: Concepts, methods, and contexts.* Washington, DC: The Aspen Institute.

Kania, J., & Kramer, M. (2011). Collective impact: Large-scale social change requires broad cross-sector coordination, yet the social sector remains focused on the isolated intervention of individual organizations. *Stanford Social Innovation Review, 9*(1).

Kubisch, A. et al. (2002). *Voices from the field II: Reflections on comprehensive community change.* Washington, DC: The Aspen Institute.

Meehan, D., Casteneda, N., & Salvesen, A. (2011). *The role of leadership in place based initiatives.* Report prepared for The California Endowment by the Leadership Learning Community. Retrieved from www.leadershiplearning.org

BETSY BAUM BLOCK *is vice president of evaluation and insight for United Way of the Bay Area, where she oversees research and evaluation for the organization's work in its seven-county region.*

NEW DIRECTIONS FOR EVALUATION • DOI: 10.1002/ev

Johnston-Goodstar, K. (2012). Decolonizing evaluation: The necessity of evaluation advisory groups in Indigenous evaluation. In R. VeLure Roholt & M. L. Baizerman (Eds.), *Evaluation advisory groups. New Directions for Evaluation, 136,* 109–117.

8

Decolonizing Evaluation: The Necessity of Evaluation Advisory Groups in Indigenous Evaluation

Katie Johnston-Goodstar

Abstract

Research was and is central to the colonization and contemporary political realities of Indigenous communities. Because evaluation is a form of research and evaluation researchers are not immune to these oppressive practices, it is essential that evaluators acknowledge and engage with this history. One way to do this is through the use of advisory groups in evaluation research. This chapter will explicate how evaluation advisory groups can help evaluation practitioners decolonize their practice. Decolonized evaluation is centered in Indigenous values and goals. It ensures that evaluation processes and outcomes are appropriate to native communities by centering Indigenous worldviews, actively including Indigenous participation, and focusing on relevance as defined by Indigenous communities. ©Wiley Periodicals, Inc., and the American Evaluation Association.

> Part of the colonization process is to render invisible the successes of indigenous science and knowledge while simultaneously infusing public discourse with images of Indians as intellectually inferior. (Walters et al., 2009, p. 148)

NEW DIRECTIONS FOR EVALUATION, no. 136, Winter 2012 © Wiley Periodicals, Inc., and the American Evaluation Association. Published online in Wiley Online Library (wileyonlinelibrary.com) • DOI: 10.1002/ev.20038

A Brief History of Research in Indigenous Communities

Research was and is central to the colonization and contemporary political realities of Indigenous communities. The word *Indigenous* refers to the communities, clans, nations, and tribes that are "Indigenous to the lands they inhabit, in contrast to and in contention with the colonial societies and states that have spread out from Europe and other centres of empire" (Alfred & Corntassel, 2005). It is used in reference to the international and intertribal collective of communities who claim this experience. In this article, the word *Indigenous* will be capitalized as a proper noun so as to acknowledge and convey respect for the political status of native tribes.

Indigenous peoples have often engaged with colonial research agendas (Smith, 1999) and research that has served to "advance the politics of colonial control" (Cochran et al., 2008, p. 22). Researchers in Indigenous communities have been involved in unethical medical experimentation, "including the removal of organs and radiation exposure" (Walters et al., 2009, p. 149), unauthorized genetic testing (Cochran et al., 2008), and the deliberate infection of Indigenous peoples with sexually transmitted diseases (Presidential Commission, 2011). Researchers have further attempted to "patent" Indigenous bodies (Smith, 1999, p. 56) and establish "pedigrees of degeneration" to argue for eugenics and sterilization policies (Gallagher, 1999; Wilson, 2002). This is how research has become "one of the dirtiest words in the indigenous world's vocabulary" (Smith, 1999, p. 1).

These dubious research practices are sadly not the only concern of Indigenous communities. According to some researchers, native peoples have been "researched to death" (Castellano, 2004) and all too often, that research provides no tangible benefits to the community. This happens so frequently, in fact, that researchers are known in tribal communities by epithets such as "drive-by" researchers (Walters et al., 2009), "mosquito" researchers (Cochran et al., 2008, p. 22), and "helicopter" researchers (Robertson, Jorgenson, & Garrow, 2004).

Because evaluation *is* a form of research, and evaluation researchers are not immune to these oppressive practices, it is essential that evaluators acknowledge and engage with this history. In native communities, research and evaluation are often indistinguishable and both are in many ways considered political acts. They are intricately tied to the colonization of the tribal community and as a consequence, researchers and evaluators must pay meticulous attention to the ways in which their practices might replicate and/or be seen to replicate these colonial patterns. This chapter will explicate how the participation of evaluation advisory groups (EAGs), commonly referred to as Community Advisory Groups in the literature on Indigenous research and evaluation methods, can help evaluation practitioners decolonize their practice and by doing so, contribute to community ownership of this type of research knowledge.

NEW DIRECTIONS FOR EVALUATION • DOI: 10.1002/ev

Nothing in this chapter should be read simply on a level of evaluation intention and perception, but rather more broadly, as a discussion about the evaluation function and practice. An awareness of colonial history in evaluation practice is essential to the practitioner, but even with awareness and the best intentions, evaluation practice remains shaped by things the evaluator may not be aware of, as well as by perceptions of evaluation held by others. Hence this chapter is deeply about method and practice, about developing a collaborative relationship within which to conduct an evaluation meaningful to community, one that meets its tests for epistemology and method as well as those of the normative evaluation practice. Moreover, although the chapter is particularly helpful to evaluation work within Indigenous communities, the information and processes herein could also benefit evaluation practitioners who work with other marginalized and culturally othered communities.

Why Evaluation Advisory Groups?

Why EAGs, one might ask? First, because Indigenous communities, quite frankly, are demanding them! Indigenous peoples and researchers have made entirely clear that they want evaluations that are "of, for, by and with us" (Kawakami, Aton, Cram, Lai, & Porima, 2007, p. 321) and research that doesn't "plan about us, without us" (Walters et al., 2009, p. 151). EAGs can work to decolonize evaluation practice through the direct involvement of community members as advisors to, and even employees of, the evaluation.

Yellow Bird (1998), in his model of the effects of colonialism, proposes the creation of "community think tanks" as an intellectual antidote to colonialism. The establishment of EAGs is one such way to create these community think tanks, which can serve to decolonize the evaluation research process. EAGs can make space for the "recovery and use of Indigenous approaches to research and evaluation, processes of knowledge creation that were once under Indigenous control but have been supplanted by Western ways of knowing" (Robertson, Jorgenson, & Garrow, 2004).

EAGs have a long tradition in many disciplines, including environmental, education, and health research. EAGs, for example, are variously defined as "made up of representatives of diverse community interests. [The] purpose is to provide a public forum for community members to present and discuss their needs and concerns" (U.S. Environmental Protection Agency, 2012) or a "dynamic group of local individuals who consult with us to make sure our work is responsive to the needs and concerns" of communities (Help Fight HIV, 2012). EAGs are particularly vital for evaluators working in Indigenous contexts because the American Evaluation Association's professional standards of *respect* states that "evaluators have the responsibility to understand and respect differences" and *competence*

NEW DIRECTIONS FOR EVALUATION • DOI: 10.1002/ev

states that evaluators must seek "awareness of their own culturally-based assumptions, their understanding of the worldviews of culturally-different participants and stakeholders in the evaluation, and the use of appropriate evaluation strategies and skills in working with culturally different groups" (American Evaluation Association, 2004). This focus on competence and respect implies that evaluators be "familiar enough with evaluation participants to be able to deliver such respect" (Kawakami et al., 2007, p. 321) and competence.

EAGs can serve to decolonize the research process and ensure the relevance of the evaluation through community-based participation. They can provide these direct benefits to the evaluation:

1. Centrality of Indigenous worldviews
2. Participatory inquiry/evaluation
3. Relevance and service to community

Centrality of Indigenous Knowledge

[D]ecolonizing research methods include deconstructing and externalizing the myth of the intellectually inferior Indian, while simultaneously privileging and centering indigenous worldviews and knowledge to promote revitalization of indigenous epistemologies, research practices, and ultimately, indigenous wellness practices. (Walters et al., 2009, p. 148)

EAGs consisting of community members who are knowledgeable about and invested in the inclusion, promotion, and practice of Indigenous worldviews are essential to decolonizing evaluation. Evaluations must consider Indigenous identity, epistemology, values, and spirituality (Kawakami et al., 2007, p. 332). Evaluations should not be designed to measure how accustomed or assimilated Indigenous tribes or programs are to Western practices. Rather, they should be situated in the "context of a specific place, time, community and history" (p. 319). They should seek to understand and measure Indigenous practice and the "value added to quality of life that the community cares about" (p. 332). In order to accomplish this, an awareness of Indigenous values and epistemologies (Meyer, 2003) in the evaluation process is necessary. EAGs can assist in this awareness and in establishing indispensable relationships that will ensure the evaluation design, implementation, relevance, and overall success of the evaluation.

Some examples that often arise in research and evaluation result from conflicting values and epistemologies. For example, many tribes place a strong value on sacred sites and spiritual practices. Because Western research and evaluation paradigms tend to see *science* and *faith* in mutually exclusive ways or in ways that prioritize science over faith, this can cause tension in the evaluation process. Western philosophies are also often anthropocentric—prioritizing humans over animal relations and sacred places, or refusing to recognize the *mana* or spiritual energy in things non-human (Johnston-Goodstar et al., 2010). Moreover, *who* holds certain knowledge, *how* that knowledge is taught/learned, and what protocols are used to *share* knowledge become critical points of contention.

Evaluations must be guided by tribal knowledge, protocols, and epistemology—in other words, the how of the knowledge should guide the evaluation (Meyer, 2001, 2003). "Knowing" in many Indigenous communities is different than in Western communities. This seemingly benign statement is particularly difficult for many evaluation researchers who are educated in institutions of higher education that promote and practice certain epistemologies without acknowledging the existence of others. Western beliefs about knowledge are often so entrenched in science that they are hard to identify, let alone wrestle with.

Indigenous values and epistemologies cannot be placed on the margins; they must be central to the evaluation process for authentic engagement and evaluation to occur. Indigenous values, protocols, and epistemologies must be respected in evaluation practices. For example, members of the HONOR Project team worked into the early morning preparing food for a kick-off feast for their new project. "[P]ersonal involvement [in values and protocols] is expected to nurture meaningful partnerships" (Walters et al., 2009, p. 147).

This is not to say that Western knowledges or practices are not welcome; indeed, many tribes see Western knowledge as complementary or helpful in their evaluation processes. But an awareness of the typical privileging of Western values, goals, and paradigms and a conscious effort to center Indigenous paradigms in the investigation of Indigenous communities is necessary to decolonizing evaluation practice.

Participatory Inquiry and Evaluation

Over the past few decades, researchers have begun to recognize how vital community participation is to research and evaluation projects. The rapid rise of community-based participatory research (Minkler & Wallerstein, 2008; Wallerstein & Duran, 2006; Walters et al., 2009) and participatory evaluation methodology is one such indication of this recognition (Checkoway & Richards-Schuster, 2003, 2004; Cousins & Whittmore, 1998). Participation is especially vital to decolonized evaluation because community members are invited to design and participate in the evaluation. Decolonized evaluation demands that the process and the results of evaluations meet the needs and desires of the community as well as those of the program and funding agencies. Local ownership of projects has been shown to "generate a sense of even greater possibility" (Robertson et al., 2004, p. 506).

The Kawakami et al. (2007) conceptual framework for Indigenous evaluation practice provides a map for participation, shaping the purpose and goals of the evaluation, the driving question/problem, the methodology, the depth and breadth of data to be collected, the analysis and recommendations of the evaluation, and the format and dissemination of findings. Indigenous evaluations are always political and moral. For example, Lakota approaches to research and evaluation support the idea of "creating knowledge in order to accomplish an end that is desired by the people" (Robertson et al., 2004, p. 500) found in the concepts of *wopasi* or inquiry and *tokata wasagle tunpi*, or something you set up to go into the future.

Participation is essential to knowing precisely what the evaluation goals, questions/problems, and methods should be. Research often frames Indigenous communities in deficit-based ways. EAGs can help to frame the inquiry in a way that asks questions pertinent to the way the community views the issues, collects suitable data for that analysis, and provides findings with real "value" (Kawakami et al., 2007, p. 331). For example: how might this evaluation help to address our questions and those "social issues" we are concerned about? In-depth participation of EAGs can also send a message to other community members that the community's opinions and participation matter to the evaluators, hence enhancing the study's credibility and utilization by decision makers for policy and program improvement and other important decisions (Cousins & Earl, 1992).

Outside evaluators may have the financial resources and Western qualifications to conduct evaluations in other communities, but a purposeful emphasis on participation allows those evaluators to share the power and "put local researchers in the driver's seat" (Robertson et al., 2004, p. 507). EAGs allow for "multiple points of entry into dialogue and gathering and confirming observations and interpretations are necessary to obtain accurate data, draw conclusions and interpret those data" (Robertson et al., 2004, p. 333). This participation is often more time-consuming and challenging to outside evaluators, but it is well worth the effort because it strengthens the validity and the relevance of the findings, explored next.

Relevance and Service to Community

EAGs are one such tool that evaluators can use to help ensure that their work holds relevance to a particular community. EAGs promote the native community standards mentioned above, but they can also assist in the analysis process, dissemination, and overall usability of the evaluation findings. This process, moreover, can help build capacity among the Indigenous community to conduct its own evaluation and research, which could potentially increase the relevance of future projects.

For example, EAGs can serve as sounding boards; they can be first to hear the findings (Kawakami et al., 2007) and provide a critical feedback loop to strengthen the data analysis or call attention to alternative or misinterpretation of findings. They can also support the dissemination of research findings through the identification of appropriate knowledge-dissemination methods (Kawakami et al., 2007). Written research reports, while valued in

Western evaluation traditions, may not always be appropriate to the community's paradigm. If story, or *mo'oelo* (narrative), *oli* (chant), or performative (tribal song) methods are most appropriate for the dissemination of the findings, then it is the evaluator's obligation to know about and use them (Lai, Yap, & Dom, 2004 cited in Kawakami et al., 2007). If evaluation findings are grounded and valid and the dissemination methods are relevant, the evaluation is more likely to be utilized. EAGs are integral to this process.

Finally, evaluation processes and outcomes that provide value to a community also help to build the capacity of those communities to conduct their own evaluations and to develop relationships for future collaborative evaluation efforts. Focusing on the relevance of the evaluation creates space to allow the community to struggle with knowledge paradigms, their own priorities in evaluation and dissemination. This struggle is key to building capacities for evaluation among community members otherwise not trained in this area, and it also allows the community to speak back to the institutions and curricula that train "evaluators."

Summary

[W]e remain a sovereign people who insist on the right to find our own solutions and our own ways of evidencing social transformations. Evaluations that support us in this effort must exhibit both academic and cultural validity. We look forward to the day when this approach becomes the norm of our evaluation experience. (Kawakami et al., 2007, p. 344)

Evaluation must be relevant to the community. It should center Indigenous knowledge paradigms and include the participation of Indigenous peoples, and it should produce outcomes and processes that are meaningful to the community and provide service to the community in a variety of negotiated ways that move beyond a cost–benefit perspective of evaluation study (Kawakami et al., 2007). Indeed, as Robertson et al. (2004) claim, evaluation should not only be relevant to a community's wants, needs, and understandings, but explicitly used in service of that community while simultaneously serving "larger goals of decolonization and liberation" (p. 500).

An evaluation study is often shaped without the knowledge or control of the Indigenous community. Until the time that Indigenous researchers and communities have full control over their own evaluation projects, EAGs are essential to complement evaluation practice. These groups can deconstruct Western assumptions, norms, and practices in order to ensure that the evaluation is centered in Indigenous epistemologies, values, and goals (Kawakami et al., 2007). They further use processes and outcomes that are appropriate to native communities by asking relevant questions and delivering relevant answers.

EAGs, however, are not only beneficial to outside evaluators. EAG participation can assist inside researchers as well. They may help call the research team's attention to mundane aspects of everyday life that may go unnoticed. They may challenge *practices as usual* that Indigenous communities have grown accustomed to, but upon further reflection counter their own decolonization, liberation, or community values. Furthermore, EAGs can provide a space for in-community variation in opinion and goals and an opportunity to dialogue further about the value of the evaluation process and the program(s) being evaluated.

References

Alfred, T., & Corntassel, J. (2005). Being Indigenous: Resurgences against contemporary colonialism. *Government and Opposition, 40*(4), 597–614.

American Evaluation Association. (2004). *Guiding principles for evaluators.* Retrieved from http://www.eval.org/publications/guidingprinciples.asp

Castellano, M. B. (2004, January). Ethics of Aboriginal research. *Journal of Aboriginal Health, 1,* 98–114.

Checkoway, B., & Richards-Schuster, K. (2003). Youth participation in community evaluation research. *American Journal of Evaluation, 24,* 21.

Checkoway, B., & Richards-Schuster, K. (2004). Youth participation in evaluation and research as a way of lifting new voices. *Children, Youth and Environments 14*(2), 84–98. Retrieved from http://www.colorado.edu/journals/cye/

Cochran, P., Marshall, C., Garcia-Downing, C., Kendell, E., Cook, D., McCubbin, L., & Gover, R. M. (2008). Indigenous ways of knowing: Implications for participatory research and community. *American Journal of Public Health, 98*(1), 22–27.

Cousins, J., & Earl, L. (1992). The case for participatory evaluation. *Educational Evaluation and Policy Analysis, 14*(4), 397–418.

Cousins, J., & Whittmore, E. (1998). Framing participatory evaluation. *New Directions for Evaluation, 80,* 5–23.

Gallagher, N. (1999). *Breeding better Vermonters: The eugenics project in the Green Mountain State.* Hanover, NH: University Press of New England.

Help Fight HIV. (2012). Community Advisory Group. Retrieved from http://www.helpfighthiv.org/board.htm

Johnston-Goodstar, K., Trinidad, A., & Tecle Solomon, A. (2010). Critical pedagogy through the reinvention of place: Two cases of youth resistance. In B. Porfilio & P. Carr (Eds.), *Youth culture, education and resistance: Subverting the commercial ordering of life.* Boston, MA: Sense Publishers.

Kawakami, A., Aton, K., Cram, F., Lai, M., & Porima, L. (2007). Improving the practice of evaluation through indigenous values and methods: Decolonizing evaluation practice—returning the gaze from Hawaii and Aotearoa. *Hulili: Multidisciplinary Research on Hawaiian Well-Being, 4*(1), 319–348.

Meyer, M. (2003). *Ho'oulu: Our time of becoming—Hawaiian epistemology and early writings.* Honolulu, HI: Ai Pohaku Press.

Meyer, M. A. (2001). Our own liberation; reflections on Hawaiian epistemology. *The Contemporary Pacific, 13*(1), 125.

Minkler, M., & Wallerstein, N. (Eds.). (2008). *Community-based participatory research for health: From process to outcomes* (2nd ed.). San Francisco, CA: Jossey-Bass.

Presidential Commission for the Study of Bioethical Issues. (2011). *"Ethically impossible": STD Research in Guatemala from 1946 to 1948.* Retrieved from www.healthequity.umd.edu/documents/Guatemala2011.pdf

Robertson, P., Jorgenson, M., & Garrow, C. (2004). Indigenizing evaluation research: How Lakota methodologies are helping "raise the Tipi" in the Oglala Sioux Nation. *American Indian Quarterly, 28*(3/4).

Smith, L.T. (1999). *Decolonizing methodologies*. London, England: Zed Books.

U.S. Environmental Protection Agency. (2012). *What is a community advisory group?* Retrieved from http://www.epa.gov/superfund/community/cag/whatis.htm

Wallerstein, N., & Duran, B. (2006). Using community-based participatory research to address health disparities. *Health Promotion Practice, 7*(3), 312–323.

Walters, K., Stately, A., Evans-Campbell, T., Simoni, J., Duran, B., Schultz, K., . . . Guerrero, D. (2009). "Indigenist" collaborative research efforts in Native American communities. In A. R. Stiffman (Ed.), *The field research survival guide.* New York, NY: Oxford University Press.

Wilson, P. (2002). Book review of Nancy L. Gallagher, *Breeding better Vermonters: The eugenics project in the Green Mountain State. Bulletin of the History of Medicine, 76,* 840–841.

Yellow Bird, M. (1998). *A model of the effects of colonialism.* Lawrence: University of Kansas, Office for the Study of Indigenous Social and Cultural Justice.

KATIE JOHNSTON-GOODSTAR *is an assistant professor, School of Social Work, University of Minnesota.*

VeLure Roholt, R. & Baizerman, M. L., (2012). A model for evaluation advisory groups: Ethos, professional craft knowledge, practices, and skills. In R. VeLure Roholt & M. L. Baizerman (Eds.), *Evaluation advisory groups. New Directions for Evaluation, 136,* 119–127.

9

A Model for Evaluation Advisory Groups: Ethos, Professional Craft Knowledge, Practices, and Skills

Ross VeLure Roholt, Michael L. Baizerman

Abstract

A practice model of evaluation advisory groups (EAGs) is described with the use of the frames of craft orientation, practice, and skills. Questions for EAG research and evaluation are presented, and a beginning guide to organizing and using an EAG is offered. A formal training agenda completes the text. © Wiley Periodicals, Inc., and the American Evaluation Association.

Evaluation advisory groups/evaluation advisory committees (EAGs/ EACs) are recommended in the evaluation literature, but are under-theorized and underdefined (Baizerman, Fink, & VeLure Roholt, 2012). Seven case studies (Block, 2012; Cohen, 2012; Compton & Baizerman, 2012; Johnston-Goodstar, 2012; Mattessich, 2012; Richards-Schuster, 2012; VeLure Roholt, 2012) provide a beginning description of how EAGs/EACs can be structured and the range of purposes they can serve for an evaluator and an evaluation project. These seven case studies were analyzed to conceptualize EAGs/EACs in three ways: first through presenting an EAG/EAC logic model; second by describing what the cases teach about the required ethos, professional craft knowledge, practices, and skills necessary for an evaluator/evaluator advisory group facilitator to have to create and manage an EAG/EAC structure and process successfully; and finally to describe the expertise of this practice. Then we use these to propose guidelines for a training curriculum and to suggest a research agenda.

Conceptualizing EAG/EAC Practice

The eight case studies were analyzed to understand the logic of how EAGs/EACs were used and to describe and better understand the practice of working with them. We begin by using a familiar evaluation tool, the logic model, to describe the logic of the EAG/EAC. (See Table 9.1.)

Inputs to EAGs/EACs include the intentional recruitment of members from different stakeholder groups (with different and sometimes overlapping areas of expertise) connected to different advice forms needed to design, complete, and use a high-quality evaluation. Who is invited to participate on an EAG/EAC depends on the needs of an evaluation study and the context in which the evaluation is taking place. Most often, EAGs/EACs provide technical advice (e.g., what design and methods to use to ensure valid and reliable data); this may not be enough for some evaluation projects, especially those in politically divisive communities (Velure Roholt & Baizerman, 2012). Here, political groups must have representation on the EAG/EAC for the evaluation to be completed. In different ways the cases describe how an EAG/EAC can provide process advice to allow an evaluator to get a study done and used effectively. Finally, an EAG/EAC can provide advice on evaluation use and can facilitate this by including relevant stakeholder groups; this too is covered in the case studies.

Centers for Disease Control (2011) describes the activities of creating and managing a required EAG/EAC in a U.S. federal context. These are supported and expanded in the case studies by Mattessich, and by Cohen, and include recruiting, vetting, and selecting members (keeping in mind size and composition of the group); orienting and training them; constructing meeting agendas; calling and facilitating meetings, clarifying purpose, leadership, and roles; regularly communicating with members; thanking them for their service at the end of the evaluation project; and evaluating the advice structure and process.

Outputs include the number and frequency of meetings, the appropriate member representation, the advice proffered by the group and by individual members, and a completed evaluation. Describing the outcomes of EAGs/EACs depends on where one wants to focus. Most often the focus is on the evaluation study, but this is not the only category of outcomes for an EAG/EAC described in the case studies. EAG/EAC also supports outcomes for stakeholders, program/community, the evaluator, and contractor. When done well, EAGs/EACs help to create better evaluations and better use of evaluations for decision making, accountability, program improvement, and/or policy development. These structures also support the credibility,

Table 9.1. Logic Model of Evaluation Advisory Groups/Evaluation Advisory Committees

Inputs	Activities	Outputs	Outcomes
Advice forms: Technical, process, and political People	Announcement Recruiting Selecting Orienting Training Creating meeting agendas Calling and facilitating meetings Rule making Clarifying purpose, leadership, and roles Communicating with members Thanking members for service	No. of meetings Stakeholders represented Advice provided Evaluation completed	**Evaluation outcomes** Better evaluation Better use of evaluation Credibility, integrity, and quality Political conciliation **Stakeholder outcomes** Involvement in creating better evaluation and in use of evaluation Support for doing an evaluation Engagement in evaluation design, process, and products **Program/community outcomes** Better services Services more utilized Ownership of evaluation process and products **Evaluator outcomes** Gain useful advice to get evaluation completed Gain entry into communities **Contractor outcomes** Better evaluation Engaged stakeholders

integrity, quality, and political reconciliation of an evaluation study. EAGs/ EACs can produce outcomes related to stakeholders, program/community members, evaluators, and contractors as well.

In addition to the often-described outcome of creating better evaluations, EAGs/EACs also provide a structure and process for stakeholder investment in an evaluation, and this in turn supports both a better evaluation and the better use of an evaluation (Patton, 1997; Weiss, 1998). Other stakeholder outcomes from EAG/EAC include increased support for the evaluation and increased engagement in the evaluation. In relation to program and community groups, EAGs/EACs can support better services, improve the use of services among community and client members, and increase ownership of the evaluation process and products by the program staff and clients and/or the community members. It also has outcomes for the evaluator and contractor.

Evaluators benefit in two primary ways. First, they are provided with useful and often necessary advice that supports the overall design, implementation, final product, and use of an evaluation. Second, as Cohen's (2012) case study describes, EAGs/EACs can provide entry into a community that otherwise would not welcome any evaluator, and even teach the evaluator how best to work in this community. Finally, EAGs/EACs create outcomes for the contractor of an evaluation study through supporting a better evaluation and increasing stakeholder engagement, and hence use. The degree to which these outcomes are achieved depends upon both the practice skill and competency of the evaluator, as is clear in the case studies. We turn to these next.

Ethos, Professional Craft Orientation and Knowledge, and Skills

The cases analyzed describe how an evaluator and an EAG/EAC facilitator can work with an EAG/EAC to create the outcomes described. We now describe the ethos, professional craft orientation and knowledge, and skills the case studies suggest as basic to creating and working effectively. Together these describe the role of an EAG/ECG facilitator, whether the evaluator or, as we prefer, an outsider.

Ethos generally refers to the "prevalent or characteristic tone" of a practice (McLaughlin, 2005, p. 311); its philosophical orientation, its value nexus. Evaluators working with EAGs/EACs understand advice as necessary, useful, as a political–moral imperative, protective, illuminative, expanding, required, taken-for-granted, doable, and educative. EAG/EAC work is serious and important and necessary to the evaluation and its uses.

Professional craft knowledge refers to the "diverse, complex and dynamic nature of knowledge derived from practice" (Titchen & Ersser, 2001, p. 36), here seen in the case studies. (See Table 9.2.)

NEW DIRECTIONS FOR EVALUATION • DOI: 10.1002/ev

Table 9.2. The Ethos, Craft Orientation and Knowledge, Practices, and Skills of the Evaluation Advisory Group/Evaluation Advisory Committee (EAG/EAC) Facilitator Role

Ethos	Commit to advice giving as necessary and achievable.
	Commit to facilitating an advice process, regardless of statute.
	Commit to the process, not to individual members or particular points of view.
	Commit to the best possible evaluation and its best possible use, under current conditions and realities.
Craft Orientation and Knowledge	Knowledge about alternative advice structures.
	Knowledge about alternative advice processes.
	Knowledge about effective meetings.
	Knowledge about effective individual consultations.
	Knowledge about individual, internal, group, organization, and interorganization politics.
Practices	The EAG/EAC facilitators are not required to know about evaluation, as such, or about the particular study they are working on; instead their focus is on how to recruit, invite, and facilitate the advice giving. They know how to put into practice what they know about (above), which is facilitating.
Skills	Working directly with individual members as experts.
	Working directly with group as an advice group.

Professional Craft Orientation, Knowledge, and Expertise

The evaluator or EAG/ECG facilitator (see below) who would construct and use an advice structure over time should know both about the following tasks and how to accomplish each. This is the facilitator's craft orientation and knowledge; it is also the evaluator's expertise. (See Table 9.3.)

Stevahn, King, Ghene, and Minnema (2005) developed a useful frame for "essential competencies for program evaluators." For our purpose, this can serve as a practical guide to the domains of expertise an evaluator can solicit from an individual (either outsider or insider), or from an advice group. Read from another perspective, included are several of the competencies needed to work with an advisory structure, but these are not included as such. If we include the basic processes of an advice structure and advice system, then the spaces for this expertise are mapped theoretically (see Baizerman, 2009, for distinctions between a competency and an expertise perspective).

New Directions for Evaluation • DOI: 10.1002/ev

Table 9.3. Outline of Major Task Sets for the EAG/ECG Facilitator

Task Sets	Specific Practices
Constructing an advice structure: external and internal; required or discretionary	Member recruitment Member screening Member vetting Member assessment Member evaluation Member retention/dismissal
Meetings: regularity, frequency, focus, leadership, records	Individual (technical assistance; consultation) Group (face-to-face, electronic, other) Premeetings Meetings Postmeeting
Evaluation of structure, process, outputs, and outcomes	Process evaluation Outcome evaluation

Following Compton and Baizerman (2009), we locate the professional craft orientation, knowledge, and expertise in the EAG/ECG facilitator role. They urge that this role be taken by someone other than the evaluator of the study. When decided otherwise, often for practical reasons, the evaluator may take on the facilitator role. In doing so, the evaluator must attend to the tensions, even the role conflicts possible, between the evaluator and facilitator role; for example, will advisors be direct and clear with their expertise if it is the evaluator who is asking for their input?

The same frame can be used to suggest a training curriculum, and it is also a base for evaluating an advice system. Research about evaluation advice structures and practices can also be conceptualized by using this frame, beginning with surveys seeking to describe existing evaluation advice structures and practices.

Training

For training, we propose additionally that attention be given to alternative modes of structure and of process, and that issues arising from tensions and disagreements between and even within professional and scholarly cultures be examined, as these can be a source limiting EAG/EAC effectiveness. "Politics"—personal, (inter) organizational, and professional—is omnipresent within groups and between members, the group, the evaluator, and the program being evaluated. Training must include extensive discussion of everyday political forms and practices for these can be mobilized to enhance the effectiveness of an EAG/EAC, but can also render it troublesome and ineffective for the evaluator.

NEW DIRECTIONS FOR EVALUATION • DOI: 10.1002/ev

Table 9.4. Examples of Technical, Process, and Use Concerns for Different Contexts of Advice

		Focus of Concern	
Advice Context	Technical Concerns	Process Concerns	Use Concerns
Soliciting advice	What technical design/method concerns do I want/ need advice on? Who has this expertise? How did I solicit this expertise? Who (what profession/discipline) would see my concerns as I do? Differently?	What is the best way to move the group forward? Can I work only with the two in the group who "get it"? Who needs to be at the table so the evaluation can be done in this context?	Who must be at the table if findings are to be used for program development?
Receiving advice	What is for me the best format for advice? Do I understand the advice? Is the timing of input OK?		
Assessing advice	Is this advice likely useful? Is it practical? Is it within my budget?		
Implementing advice	How do I put this advice into play at this stage? Is my staff able to implement this advice?		
Evaluating the advice	Did the advice work? Was it a wise choice? Should I have kept soliciting ideas?		

Another training focus should be on working with a small group. At best, this expertise is invisible when members work well as a group; when the group is ineffective, it is likely that the facilitator's group skills are poor (we are aware that ineffective groups can result from member selection, group-member interpersonal chemistry, substantive disagreement, and other nonpersonal or interpersonal sources).

Two final training foci could include the advice system as such and types of concern and related types of expertise. These types of concern were identified in the literature review: technical (about evaluation design and methods), process (about evaluation implementation), and use (about using the study and its findings). Also discussed were the four stages of an advice system: Soliciting advice, receiving input, assessing input, and implementing the advice. We add here a fifth: evaluating the advice and advice system. Both of these topics are basic to EAG/ECG work. They can be treated independently or together, as in the example given in Table 9.4.

Effective Advice

Argyris (2000) studied advice given to managers. His criteria for effective (and by extension poor) advice ends this volume.

- Advice is effective to the extent that it is valued and actionable—that is, leads to effective action.
- There are three tests for the validity of advice. If implemented correctly, it leads to the consequences it predicts will occur; its effectiveness persists so long as no unforeseen conditions interfere; and it can be implemented and tested in the world of everyday practice.
- There are four tests for the actionability of advice. It specifies the detailed, concrete behaviors required to achieve the intended consequences; it must be crafted in the form of designs that contain causal statements; people must have, or be able to be taught, the concepts and skills required to implement those causal statements; and the context in which it is to be implemented does not prevent its implementation (p. 79).

Therefore, "for advice to be helpful, it must specify the intended outcomes or objectives to be produced, the sequence of actions required to produce them, the actions required to monitor and test for any errors or mistakes" (Argyris, 2000, p. 9).

References

Argyris, C. (2000). *Flawed advice and the management trap*. New York, NY: Oxford University Press.

Baizerman, M., Fink, A., & VeLure Roholt, R. (2012). From consilium to advice: A review of the evaluation and related literature on advisory structures and processes.

In R. VeLure Roholt & M. L. Baizerman (Eds.), *Evaluation advisory groups. New Directions for Evaluation, 136,* 5–29.

Block, B. B. (2012). Congratulations on the new initiative! Is it time for a new committee? In R. VeLure Roholt & M. L. Baizerman (Eds.), *Evaluation advisory groups. New Directions for Evaluation, 136,* 101–108.

Centers for Disease Control and Prevention (CDC) Division of Nutrition, Physical Activity, and Obesity. (2011). *Developing and using an evaluation consultation group.* Atlanta, GA: CDC.

Cohen, B. B. (2012). Advisory groups for evaluations in diverse cultural groups, communities, and contexts. In R. VeLure Roholt & M. L. Baizerman (Eds.), *Evaluation advisory groups. New Directions for Evaluation, 136,* 49–65.

Compton, D., & Baizerman, M. (2009). Managing program evaluation: Towards explicating a professional practice. *New Directions for Evaluation, 121.*

Compton, D. W., & Baizerman, M. L. (2012). The evolution of a philosophy and practice of evaluation advice. In R. VeLure Roholt & M. L. Baizerman (Eds.), *Evaluation advisory groups. New Directions for Evaluation, 136,* 67–76.

Johnston-Goodstar, K. (2012). Decolonizing evaluation: The necessity of evaluation advisory groups in Indigenous evaluation. In R. VeLure Roholt & M. Baizerman (Eds.), *Evaluation advisory groups. New Directions for Evaluation, 136,* 109–117.

Mattessich, P. W. (2012). Advisory committees in contract and grant-funded evaluation projects. In R. VeLure Roholt & M. L. Baizerman (Eds.), *Evaluation advisory groups. New Directions for Evaluation, 136,* 31–48.

McLaughlin, T. (2005). The educative importance of ethos. *The British Journal of Educational Studies, 53*(3), 306–325.

Patton, M. Q. (1997). *Utilization-focused evaluation: The new century text.* Thousand Oaks, CA: Sage Publishing.

Richards-Schuster, K. (2012). Empowering the voice of youth: The role of youth advisory councils in grant making focused on youth. In R. VeLure Roholt & M. L. Baizerman (Eds.), *Evaluation advisory groups. New Directions for Evaluation, 136,* 87–100.

Stevahn, L., King, J. A., Ghene, G., & Minnema, J. (2005). Establishing essential competencies for program evaluators. *American Journal of Evaluation, 26,* 43–59.

Titchen, A., & Ersser, S. (2001). The nature of professional craft knowledge. In J. Higgs & A. Titchen (Eds.), *Practice knowledge and expertise in the health professions* (pp. 35–41). Oxford, England: Butterworth-Heinemann.

VeLure Roholt, R. (2012). Advice giving in contested space. In R. VeLure Roholt & M. L. Baizerman (Eds.), *Evaluation advisory groups. New Directions for Evaluation, 136,* 77–85.

VeLure Roholt, R., & Baizerman, M. (2012). Being practical, being safe: Doing evaluations in contested spaces. *Evaluation and Program Planning, 35*(1), 206–217.

Weiss, C. (1998). *Evaluation* (2nd ed.). Upper Saddle River, NJ: Prentice-Hall Publishers.

ROSS VELURE ROHOLT *is an assistant professor in the School of Social Work, University of Minnesota.*

MICHAEL L. BAIZERMAN *is a professor in the School of Social Work, University of Minnesota.*

INDEX

ORDER FORM SUBSCRIPTION AND SINGLE ISSUES

DISCOUNTED BACK ISSUES:

Use this form to receive 20% off all back issues of *New Directions for Evaluation*.
All single issues priced at **$23.20** (normally $29.00)

TITLE	ISSUE NO.	ISBN
_____	_____	_____
_____	_____	_____
_____	_____	_____

Call 888-378-2537 or see mailing instructions below. When calling, mention the promotional code JBNND to receive your discount. For a complete list of issues, please visit www.josseybass.com/go/ev

SUBSCRIPTIONS: (1 YEAR, 4 ISSUES)

☐ New Order   ☐ Renewal

U.S.	☐ Individual: $89	☐ Institutional: $313
CANADA/MEXICO	☐ Individual: $89	☐ Institutional: $353
ALL OTHERS	☐ Individual: $113	☐ Institutional: $387

Call 888-378-2537 or see mailing and pricing instructions below.
Online subscriptions are available at www.onlinelibrary.wiley.com

ORDER TOTALS:

Issue / Subscription Amount: $ _____

Shipping Amount: $ _____
(for single issues only – subscription prices include shipping)

Total Amount: $ _____

SHIPPING CHARGES:
First Item $6.00
Each Add'l Item $2.00

(No sales tax for U.S. subscriptions. Canadian residents, add GST for subscription orders. Individual rate subscriptions must be paid by personal check or credit card. Individual rate subscriptions may not be resold as library copies.)

BILLING & SHIPPING INFORMATION:

☐ **PAYMENT ENCLOSED:** *(U.S. check or money order only. All payments must be in U.S. dollars.)*

☐ **CREDIT CARD:**   ☐VISA   ☐MC   ☐AMEX

Card number _____Exp. Date_____

Card Holder Name_____Card Issue # _____

Signature _____Day Phone_____

☐ **BILL ME:** *(U.S. institutional orders only. Purchase order required.)*

Purchase order # _____
Federal Tax ID 13559302 • GST 89102-8052

Name _____

Address_____

Phone_____ E-mail_____

Copy or detach page and send to: **John Wiley & Sons, One Montgomery Street, Suite 1200, San Francisco, CA 94104-4594**

Order Form can also be faxed to: **888-481-2665**

PROMO JBNND